D1396019

Crimes of the Community

HONOUR-BASED VIOLENCE IN THE UK.

by
James Brandon and Salam Hafez

2008

CENTRE FOR SOCIAL COHESION

Crimes of the Community:
Honour-based violence in the UK
by
James Brandon and Salam Hafez

Centre for Social Cohesion
A Civitas Project

Centre for Social Cohesion
Clutha House
10 Storey's Gate
London SW1P 3AY
Tel: +44 (0)20 7222 8909
Fax: +44 (0)5 601527476
Email: mail@socialcohesion.co.uk
www.socialcohesion.co.uk

Director:
Douglas Murray

The Centre for Social Cohesion is a Civitas project
CIVITAS is a registered charity: No. 1085494.
Limited by guarantee.
Registered in England and Wales: No. 04023541

© Centre for Social Cohesion, January 2008
All the Institute's publications seek to further its objective of promoting the advancement of learning.
The views expressed are those of the authors,
not of the Institute.
Crimes of the community: Honour-based violence in the UK

All rights reserved

ISBN 978-1-903386-64-4

Printed in Great Britain by
The Cromwell Press
Trowbridge, Wiltshire

Contents

CHAPTER 5

CHAPTER 6

CHAPTER 8

Recomendations: how the government can accelerate change

CHAPTER 9

Conclusion

Introduction

In recent years, honour crimes have received an increasing amount of interest from the media, the police and politicians. This has been fuelled by the extensive coverage of the murder of several young Kurdish and Pakistani women by their families.[1] This growing public concern has been largely welcomed by women's groups and has prompted the government to take steps to tackle these crimes. However the media's focus on honour killings and, to a lesser extent, forced marriages and Female Genital Mutilation (FGM) has obscured the true scale of honour-based crime. Honour killings represent only the tip of the iceberg in terms of violence and abuse perpetrated against women in the name of honour.

This study shows that honour killings, domestic violence, forced marriage and FGM are not isolated practices but are instead part of a self-sustaining social system built on ideas of honour and cultural, ethnic and religious superiority. As a result of these ideas, every day around the UK women are being threatened with physical violence, rape, death, mutilation, abduction, drugging, false imprisonment, withdrawal from education and forced marriage by their own families. This is not a one-time problem of first-generation immigrants bringing practices from 'back home' to the UK. Instead honour violence is now, to all intents and purposes, an indigenous and self-perpetuating phenomenon which is carried out by third and fourth generation immigrants who have been raised and educated in the UK.

This report focuses on four aspects of honour-based violence:

- ■ *Forced marriage*

- ■ *Domestic violence*

- ■ *Honour killings*

---

1 Some of the most frequently cited killings have been those of Rukhsana Naz, a 19-year old woman of Pakistani origin in Derby in 1998, Heshu Yones, a 16-year old Kurdish girl in North London in 2003, and Banaz Mahmod, a 20-year old Kurdish woman in South London in 2006. *The Guardian*: 'Love, honour and obey – or die', by Jason Burke. October 8 2000. http://observer.guardian.co.uk/international/story/0,6903,379174,00.html

■ *Female Genital Mutilation*

Many of these problems are common to all societies. Domestic violence and 'crimes of passion' exist worldwide. However, honour crimes differ significantly from other outwardly similar crimes. While typical incidents of domestic violence involve men using force against their wives, honour-based abuses regularly involve a woman's own sons, brothers and sisters, as well as members of their extended family and in-laws. Similarly, the pre-planned and ritualised nature of much of this violence (particularly in the case of honour-killings and FGM) makes such behaviour distinct from other ad-hoc forms of violence against women.

This study explains how and why many British women, and indeed many men, are told that they are not allowed the right to be independent, to have control over their own bodies and who are being denied, often through force, an opportunity to choose their own destiny. The report concludes with recommendations on what the government can do to prevent these abuses.

CHAPTER 1

Origins of honour

Introduction

Honour is a fluid concept which has been widely interpreted by different societies, cultures and classes throughout history to promote behaviour which is seen as beneficial to the community. At various times honour has been equated with attributes as diverse as bravery or cunning, strength or wisdom, vengefulness or mercy. In all societies, honour has both a private and a public aspect. On one hand it describes an individual's 'self-respect'; how a person sees himself and his relative value in society. But at the same time, measures of honour also dictate the extent to which society accepts a person's self-worth and help determine the level of status and material benefits which it accords him as a result.

Sexual honour

The form of honour dealt with in this study arises from ideas that the reputation and social standing of an individual, a family or a community is based on the behaviour and morality of its female members. Like other forms of honour, this concept does not exist in a vacuum but rather as a central part of a complex social structure which governs relationships between different families, genders and social units within a given society.

■ The origins of an idea

Anthropologists have suggested a number of reasons for the development of ideas that the honour of an individual or a group is determined by the behaviour of women. Many speculate that this behaviour evolved because early man wanted to be sure that the children he helped raise, gathered food for and protected were carrying his genes. The most obvious way for him to do this was to ensure that 'his' woman did not have sex either immediately prior to or after his coupling with her. Therefore, researchers suggest, men who controlled their women came to be seen as strong, high-status leaders of society; able to prey on the sexual partners of other men but keeping their own women chaste and apart.[2]

Others have argued that a sexualised form of honour developed because early societies viewed women as a form of property which could be traded for other commodities. As a result, women's bodies and sexuality gained a monetary value which in turn encouraged their husbands and family to regulate their sexual behaviour and to guard it as they would any other form of capital. The anthropologist Ladislav Holy, for example, wrote that in such societies, "honour is a similar resource to property, economic cooperation or power. It too has to be secured and protected in the same way as these other resources."[3] Where such societies had a strong tribal component, women's bodies also became a commodity held in common by her relatives who all stood to benefit collectively from the alliances and profits that could be gained from the marriage of an eligible virgin to members of other tribes and families. As patriarchal notions of morality and culture deepened, these idealisations of a woman's sexual behaviour gradually came to be enforced through dress codes and cultural notions of 'right' and 'wrong'. As societies developed further, men were able to embed ideas of honour in culture by asserting their right to be the civil, political and economic leaders of society at the expense of women. In almost all cases, this male domination of a society's religious, judicial and cultural spheres institutionalised the subordination of women to her husband and other male relatives – despite the key role that women traditionally played in creating wealth through their working in agriculture and primitive industries such as weaving and textile production. Over time, men's ability to uphold these ideas of 'proper' female behaviour and ensure that women conformed to these social norms became equated with their own social standing, status and 'honour'. Upholding the honour of men and women therefore became dependent on restricting women's actions, behaviour and thoughts.

■ Honour today

Until recently, similar concepts of honour were found across the UK and throughout much of Europe. Today, however, such extreme and overtly articulated forms of sexualised honour in the UK primarily exist among immigrants and their descendents from the Middle East and South Asia, although such sentiments

---

2 See, for example, Ladislav Holy, *Kinship: Honour and Solidarity: Cousin marriage in the Middle East* (Manchester University Press, Manchester, 1989), Amina Wahud's *Inside the Gender Jihad: Women's Reform in Islam* (Oneworld Publications, Oxford, 2006) and JG Peristiany (ed.) *Honour and Shame: The values of Mediterranean Society* (University of Chicago, Chicago 1966; London 1974).

3 Ladislav Holy *Honour and Shame: The Values of Mediterranean Society* ed. by Jean G. Peristiany (Chicago University Press, Chicago, 1966) p. 75

also exist among sectors of the Afro-Caribbean and Latin American population, as well as among portions of the white English populace.[4] However, the idea of honour as found among Middle Eastern and Asian immigrants in the UK is often distinctive because it is openly expressed, and because it has arguably become the basis for organising such communities as well as playing an important part of many people's cultural and religious identities. Just as any honour-based society has always granted social and material advantages to those who conform, so is the case in such communities in the UK today.

Advantages of honour

❖ **Self-awareness/pride**

In societies which are ordered around ideas of honour, upholding perceived standards of behaviour can become the basis of a person's identity and positive self-image.

❖ **Increased security and prospects for offspring**

Families which conform to accepted standards of honour and moral behaviour receive benefits in terms of a better future for their sons who enjoy increased marriage and career prospects within their community.

❖ **Improved contacts and business opportunities**

Families which publicly uphold their honour usually gain increased social status. This can result in better contacts within the community which can lead to material benefits such as increased income for the self-employed and greater trade for owners of shops and businesses.

❖ **Providing stability in an changing/new environment**

For immigrants arriving in the UK, vesting one's identity in intangibles such as traditional ideas of honour and pride can be safer than rooting one's reputation and social worth in terms of property, wealth and a career.

❖ **Sense of superiority (vis-à-vis members of other ethnic groups, castes, religions)**

For immigrants with low career prospects, investing in ideas of sexual honour can provide a way to feel superior to strangers by measuring

---

4 For example, although honour killings are usually understood as murders of women committed by close family members from Asian or Middle Eastern backgrounds, there is reason to believe that many murders by whites could also be classed as 'honour killings'. For instance, the Home Office report 'Violence crime overview, homicide and gun crime 2004/5' found that of the 231 women murdered during that period, 14 percent were killed by family members (not including partners or ex-partners). http://www.homeoffice.gov.uk/rds/pdfs06/hosb0206.pdf

oneself against a different value scale based on ideas of honour and 'proper' moral behaviour.

Among Middle Eastern and South Asian immigrants in the UK, there are many ways in which a person can bring shame and dishonour on themselves and their family.

Common ways in which honour can be damaged

❖ **Defying parental authority**
In many cultures, elder members of the family are expected to control their children. Parents who publicly fail to do so may lose status in the community as a result.

❖ **Becoming 'western' (clothes, behaviour, attitude)**
People from honour-based cultures often transform ideas of honour into a pride in one's origins and/or religion once they settle in 'the West'. Families who allow their children to assimilate into wider society can be seen as betraying their origins, their community and their ancestors.

❖ **Women having sex/relationships before marriage**
Many honour-based cultures put a high premium on a girl's virginity and sexual fidelity. Families whose women are believed to have extramarital relationships (even of a non-sexual kind) can suffer a decline in honour and social standing.

❖ **Use of drugs or alcohol**
Drinking alcohol and using drugs not endorsed by religion, culture or tradition can bring shame on families because their children are seen as abandoning or rejecting the values of their parents and their community.

❖ **Gossip**
In many cases honour is damaged less by a person's action than by knowledge of that action becoming public knowledge. Rumours and gossip – even if untrue – can damage the status of a family or an individual.

In many cases, families are less concerned with immoral acts, than with how these will affect how they are seen by their relatives and by other members of their community. As honour is an intangible asset dependent on a community's perceptions, an 'immoral' act does not become 'shameful' or 'dishonourable' until it becomes public knowledge. The consequences of damaging one's honour or the honour of one's family can be serious.

KEY MIDDLE EASTERN AND SOUTH ASIAN WORDS RELATED TO HONOUR

Ird: (Arab countries) *Ird* also expresses how the honour of a man, family or community is vested in their women. A woman is born with *ird*, which is best understood as sexual purity. Once it is taken away or damaged it cannot be restored. However unlike virginity, a woman retains her *ird* after marriage. *Ird* is voided by sexual conduct which the community deems to be wrong or which transgresses traditional standards of behaviour.

Izzat: (mainly South Asia) *Izzat* usually refers to the collective honour of a family, community or even a country. The behaviour of this group's women is seen as one of the main threats to *izzat*. In Pakistan's Punjab region, *Ghairat*, has a similar meaning, combining concepts of honour, jealousy, courage, modesty and shame, which can apply to both men and women. *Be-ghairat*, shamelessness, refers to those without a sense of honour.

Namus: (Pakistan, Turkey, Kurdistan and Iran) *Namus* describes how the honour of men or of a family is dependent on the dependent of their females. Derived from the Greek *nomos*, *namus* is additionally used to describe traditional modes of behaviour which are seen as compatible with Islam. In Turkish numerous words are closely related to *namus*. For example, *Namusa laf gelmek* translates as other people's gossip about one's *namus* – a possible pretext for violence. *Namusu kirlenmek* or *lekelenmek* refers to one's *namus* being dirtied or stained, and *namusunu temizlemek* to a man's attempt (and obligation) to clean it. *Namussuz*, the most damaging concept of all, signals a total loss of *namus*.

Zina: (Muslim world) *Zina* is the word used in the Quran to describe extra-marriage sexual relations. The Quran specifies that punishments for *zina* are enacted in both the afterlife and under Sharia law. Some States which apply forms of Sharia law stipulate punishments such as lashing, imprisonment or stoning to death for *zina*.

Other related words:

Sharam: (South Asia) *Sharam* refers to how a woman is expected to behave. Ideas of acceptable, honourable, behaviour usually include modest dress and behaviour and subservience to one's male relatives.

Sharaf: (Arab world) *Sharaf* is used to denote a man's sense of honour and self-worth. If he fails to control the behaviour of his female relatives, his *sharaf* may be damaged.

Pride: Many third-generation immigrants from South Asia brought up in the UK now use the words such as pride or respect to describe how the behaviour of women reflects of their families and communities.

Consequences of losing one's honour include:

❖ Ostracism by family and community

Families whose honour has been damaged can be ignored and ostracised by other members of the community. Their children may also be rejected at school by fellow members of their cultural, ethnic or religious group.

❖ Economic damage

Families whose honour is damaged may receive smaller dowries for their children. In extreme cases, their shops and businesses can also be boycotted or even physically attacked by community members who believe that their collective honour has also been damaged.

❖ Political consequences

Community leaders and politicians from honour-based communities whose honour is damaged can lose votes, prestige and influence as a result.

❖ Loss of self-esteem

Members of families whose honour is damaged can become depressed, suicidal or abusive. Feelings of shame can hamper their interactions with other members of their community and can negatively affect their work, possibly causing further damage to their social standing as a result.

To avoid the serious consequences that can result from losing one's honour, individuals, families and communities may take drastic steps to preserve, protect or avenge their honour. This can lead to substantial human rights abuses including forced marriage, domestic violence, honour killing and female genital mutilation. The prevalence of such different forms of honour-based violence varies from community to community, depending on each group's cultural, social and religious traditions.

CHAPTER 2

Forced Marriage

Introduction

Ghazala Razzaq, co-ordinator at Roshni Asian Women's Resource Centre, an advice and training centre in Sheffield, says:

66 There is pressure on parents from the immediate family; it is a matter of honour; there is a feeling that the father must be in control of the family. Promises are also made by parents to their immediate family. Men from England go back to Asia as they want a docile wife to care for them and do the cooking and cleaning 99

The practice of forcing women into marriage through threats of violence is common among many communities in the UK. British police define a forced marriage as "a marriage conducted without valid consent of one or both parties, where duress is a factor".[5] According to most definitions, a marriage becomes forced if any coercion, physical or psychological, used against either spouses in order to force them to consent. A forced marriage is not the same as an arranged marriage which occurs with the full consent of both parties. The Forced Marriage Unit,[6] run jointly by the Foreign and Commonwealth Office and the Home Office deals with an average of 300 cases of forced marriages every year, some of whom have involved girls as young as 13. However, women's groups and police say the total number of cases of forced marriage is much higher.

Forced marriages can occur in almost any community governed by honour, pride and shame. Such communities include South Asians, Kurds, Arabs, Iranians, Turks and, in some cases, ultra-orthodox Jewish communities among others. Some women's groups also report they have encountered forced marriages among white British communities. However, most workers in women's refuges say that the majority of people who use their services to escape an arranged marriage are Pakistani. Shaminder Ubhi, director of Ashiana, a women's refuge in Leyton, East London, says:

"Forced marriage exists mostly in South Asian communities because of the size of the population and the services that are provided for women fleeing such cases. However, the problem of forced marriage is also high in other communities such as the Turkish and Kurdish. To some extent there is more awareness with the Asian community; the women's sector has been established for the last few years; more refuges and services and a lot more awareness now exists in the commu-

---

5 For further details on police definition of forced marriage: http://www.gmp.police.uk/mainsite/pages/forcedmarriage.htm

6 Forced Marriage Unit (FMU), *Tackling Human Rights Abuses* http://www.fco.gov.uk/servlet/Front?pagename=OpenMarket/Xcelerate/ShowPage&c=Page&cid=1094234857863

nity especially since the government's forced marriage report which
was published in 1999."

Extreme violence is often used to force individuals into marriages
which will produce social or material benefits for the family. Forcing a person into marriage does not necessarily require physical
violence. Families (usually parents but in some cases members of
the extended family) will often use psychological abuse, blackmail and threats of imprisonment to force their children to accept
a marriage. In extreme cases, victims have been forcibly taken
back to their native countries where more extreme violence may
be used against them. Forced marriages do not only happen to
women. According to police figures, 15 per cent of those forced
into marriage are men.[7] Amtal Rana, project worker at Kiran
Asian Women's Aid in Leytonstone in East London, says:

> "Boys are also pressurised to marry. My cousin got pressured to marry
> someone even when he didn't want to, but eventually gave his con-
> sent because he thought he'd go with it in the hope that the marriage
> would change. But in the end they divorced and two lives were ru-
> ined! The marriage lasted seven to eight months."

Although forced marriages appear to be most common among
South Asians, women from other communities can also be forced
to marry cousins and members of their tribe and extended family to reinforce kinship networks, their family's business ties and
tribal alliances. Diana Nammi, the director of the Iranian and
Kurdish Women's Rights Organisation, a refuge and advice centre in East London, says:

> "In Kurdish culture this is also a tribal issue. A lot of people believe
> their daughter has to marry from among the same tribe ... [Kurdish]
> communities are very closed. Some of those communities have be-
> come like ghettos. Marriage and so on is only done between families.
> It becomes a way of keeping their culture and religion and of being in
> opposition to Western culture."

Not all honour-based communities suffer from forced marriage.
Omar Yasin Ibrahim, an advice worker at the Islington Somali
Community Centre in London, says that he has not come across
any cases of forced marriage among the UK's Somali community:

> "Forced marriage happens in Somalia but the practice does not exist
> outside of the country, so in England the community is fine. How-

---

7 *BBC*: 'Police urge forced marriage law'. 21 March 2005. http://news.bbc.co.uk/1/hi/
uk/4367087.stm

Number of spouses given visas to enter the UK per year.		
Number of husbands entering Britain		
	1996	*2006*
Indian sub-continent:	3,540	6,320
African:	710	3,025
Middle East:	340	1,275
Overall total:	6,460	14,295
Number of wives entering Britain		
	1996	*2006*
Indian sub-continent:	5,740	10,045
African:	1,070	3,680
Middle East:	1,880	7,215
Overall total number:	12,200	26,665
Source: Control of Immigration: Statistics, United Kingdom, 2006 (HMSO, 2007)		

ever, some Asian women refuges have had nominal cases of Somali women."

Fathiya Yusuf, the Somali community outreach worker for Refuge in South East London, says:

"We don't have this problem in the Somali community. But we have semi-arranged marriages where a person is not forced but is pressured to marry a second-cousin or someone from the same tribe. In my experience in Somalia even in the most rural countryside forced marriage isn't an issue like it is in the Asian community here."

However, some activists say that they are dealing with an increasing number of forced marriages are occurring in communities that have not been previously associated with the practice. Ila Patel, director of the Asha Project, a refuge in Streatham in South London, says:

Ila Patel, director of the Asha Project, a refuge in Streatham in South London, says:

66 I was talking to Lambeth Women's Aid, and they were saying that forced marriage referrals from African and Eastern European communities are on the increase 99

"I was talking to Lambeth Women's Aid, and they were saying that forced marriage referrals from African and Eastern European communities are on the increase. So that is something that we are looking at as well."

Although the nature and extent of forced marriage can differ between different communities, in many cases the motives for forcing men and women into marriages are often very similar.

Motives for forced marriage

Forced marriages can occur for a variety of reasons which are frequently linked to upholding honour-based traditions.[8] Often parents force their children to marry in order to control their sexual behaviour and to pre-empt any actions that could shame the family. In other cases, however, families use forced marriage to strengthen family, community and caste ties and preserve and maintain the family's material wealth.

In many cases, forced marriages are carried out to prevent or limit the influence of 'western' ideas on children from traditional backgrounds who are brought up in the UK. Humera Khan, co-founder of An-Nisa Society, a women's advocacy group based in Wembley, says:

> "It is natural for parents to try and replicate something that is natural to them. The roots of all forced marriage is fear; fear of 'western' culture that they see as something that is against what they are and which is appealing to the young people – particularly to their sexual desire. They are a little bit scared of that; and rather than equipping their children with the skills to navigate through these two cultures they are living in, they want to take away their responsibility and get them married off so that it is over and done with."

In many communities, families can force their daughters to marry members of their own community if they are dating or planning to marry someone from another community. Gona Saed, director of Middle East Centre for Women's Rights, says:

> "There is suspicion of any outsiders. One very big issue around forced marriage is Sharia law and marrying a non-Muslim. In Islamic Sharia law a Muslim woman is strictly forbidden to marry a non-Muslim. For example, if a girl falls in love with a guy at college and he is not a Muslim, the family will object to the marriage, definitely. They will probably force her to stop seeing him and marry someone else."

Many communities have social and cultural penalties for those who marry members of other groups. Such people are often perceived as 'betraying' their religion, ancestors and heritage. Abigail Morris, director of Jewish Women's Aid, a women's refuge in North London, says:

> "It's called 'Marrying Out'; it's a 'you're in or you're out' kind of thing. In the more extreme communities they do prayers as if you have died

---

8 *Foreign Commonwealth Office*: 'Dealing with Cases of Forced Marriage': http://www.fco.gov.uk/Files/kfile/forcedmarriageguidelines.pdf

C A S E   S T U D Y

A TEENAGER WHO ESCAPED A FORCED MARRIAGE

'Sakina' is a 19 years old woman of Pakistani origin who was born and brought up in the UK. She has run away from home twice in order to escape being forced into marriage. She is presently living in a refuge in the Midlands:

I first left home on March 19th. My dad wanted to get me married. So I ran away. First I went to Walsall and I stayed there. But then I went back home. At first my dad was 'everything will be alright'. After a few days though my dad said 'we're going to Pakistan'. I was like 'forget that', so I ran away again. I said I was going to go visit my gran's – this was at about eight at night – and before I did I packed up my clothes and threw them in a bag and threw them out of the window into the garden. Then I went out of the front door, got my stuff and disappeared off to the station. Half-an-hour later my dad found out that I'd gone. This time I stayed at a cousin's.

The guy I was supposed to get married to was my cousin. I saw him for the first time on a video. It was video of another wedding and he was in it. My mother said 'that's him – that's the one you're going to marry. You're gonna marry him, you are'. Since such a young age you get told that you'll get married. You think that it worked out for everyone else and so it'll work out for you. But I told my parents 'no, I don't want to get married' and they didn't listen. My mum said 'what's wrong with my cousins?' They put the guilt on you.

Because I didn't get married to him, they gave him my sister instead – that's what it's like. She's in Pakistan now. She's 16 and she's pregnant. They had promised me verbally to him and his family when I was born. But now because I've run away they've given my sister to him instead. My sister blames me because she's in this situation – she's three months pregnant and has been married for four months. My dad won't bring her back 'til she's had the baby. He's afraid that she'll have an abortion. It doesn't matter to them what happens to her – they got what they wanted – they got the land that his family had. I think my dad would have let me marry who I wanted but he listened my mother and her family. The thing that I don't get is that my dad was brought up in this country and he had arranged marriage himself.

After I ran away I wasn't in touch with my family for four or five months But now I speak to my family; and my mum and my grandparents – but not to my dad. They've got this idea that I'll come back and we'll all play happy families but no way, no way. They think that because you've run away once that you'll run away again. They don't trust you. After I went back I wasn't allowed out; I wasn't allowed to do anything. The community thinks that if you do a runner that you're sleeping around. If you come back they say 'who have you been with then?' Sometimes you think 'why have I come here; why did I leave my home'.

Sometimes I think maybe I'll just go back and do whatever they say – just because it's easier. Now my parents want me back. One day I might want to go back and they'll just say 'no, we asked you to come back and you didn't want to come and now it's too late and now we don't want you'. Most of the family is fine with me. I just don't talk to my dad. My mum's got it in her head that because I've been back before I'll go back again.

called 'Shivu'; they would act as if the person had died, do the prayer and then never speak of them again. "

In many cases, especially among South Asians, women are forced to marry first cousins. Families often do this to protect the family's wealth or to reaffirm familial ties. Shaminder Ubhi, director of Ashiana Women's Aid, a women's refuge in Leyton, says:

"Sometimes [forced marriage] is about forming a partnership with another family and sometimes parents agree with the other family from
a young age that cousins will marry as a kind of deal. Once a promise
has been made then the family will do the utmost to honour that deal
and make it happen."

In addition to keeping promises made to relatives abroad, many
South Asian men brought up in the UK want to marry uneducated women (often known as a 'freshie') who are 'uncontami-
nated' by ideas of female independence. Ghazala Razzaq, co-ordinator at Roshni Asian Women's Resource Centre, an advice
and training centre in Sheffield, says:

"There is pressure on parents from the immediate family; it is a matter
of honour; there is a feeling that the father must be in control of the
family. Promises are also made by parents to their immediate family.
Men from England go back to Asia as they want a docile wife to care
for them and do the cooking and cleaning."

In some cases, families will also seek to forcibly marry men
brought up in the UK to women from traditional families 'back
home' in order to cure their 'western' attitudes – although this
practice is rare. Imran Rehman, a 33-year old support worker at
Karma Nirvana, a refuge in Derby, was taken from Birmingham
to Pakistan to be forcibly married when he was 17. He says that,
in his case, the marriage was arranged not only because he was
becoming 'westernised' but because he was involved in drugs
and crime. He says:

"Police were knocking on my door every other week and so my mum
said 'send him to Pakistan'. Mum could see all the trouble that I was
causing and that I needed rehabilitating. She knew that this was a way
to cure me or otherwise I'd get locked up."

Shahien Taj, the director of the Henna Foundation, an advice and
advocacy centre in Cardiff, says that families can be so keen for
conservative men born abroad to come to enforce traditional values on their female children, that marriages are even conducted
over the phone and, sometimes, via recorded video messages.
She says:

"I have a young mother who came in to the office and said that she
wanted to get her daughter married to her nephew in Pakistan. She
said 'I'd rather the marriage takes place on the phone'. She asked is
there a way to get the husband over by doing 'Nikah' on the phone
and is it a problem that her daughter is only 16. She said that her relatives in Cardiff, Birmingham, Sheffield and Bradford are all rushing to
Pakistan to marry their daughters as we speak so that they can get their

Philip Balmforth, the vulnerable persons'
officer (Asian women) for the police in
Bradford, says:

66 There are thousands of people
in Bradford from Mirpur, who
would be poor people living in a
village in Pakistan. One family is
an entire village, so you get this
ghetto society in that village of
people living off each other and
everybody knows each other. So with
the forced marriage situation, they
would marry within each other to
keep the family together and their
possessions together, like land and
wealth in case of death. It is all
about the honour of that village, so
the next village down the road says,
'oh look at that village, look how
good they are' 99

applications in before March 2008[when the government may raise the age limit for overseas marriages from 19 to 21]."

In some cases, forced marriages are carried out so that families will have a cheap source of domestic labour. In some towns in northern England, men are brought from abroad to work long hours on less-than minimum wages in businesses owned by their in-laws. Zalkha Ahmed, director of Apna Haq, a women's support group, says:

"We have a lot of them here and they are mainly used as cheap slave labour and domestic workers."

The motives for forced marriage can include:

❖ **Maintain the family's honour and pride in the eyes of the community**

❖ **Strengthen family ties with the community or extended family; sometimes in order to improve the family's financial position**

❖ **Control the behavioural patterns in order to comply with the traditional norms of one's family or community**

❖ **Preserve and maintain the family's wealth, which is often in the family's native country**

❖ **Prevent relationships with individuals from outside one's ethnic, cultural, religious group or caste**

❖ **Assist relatives immigrating to the UK**

❖ **Fulfil long-standing family commitments and promises**

❖ **Maintain the order of marriage within siblings (in many cases it is customary for the oldest sibling to marry first)**

Abuses related to forced marriage

Many women who are being forced into marriage suffer from physical and emotional violence. In the period leading up to a forced marriage, young women are often withdrawn from school and can be imprisoned. This isolation from the outside world is often accompanied by physical violence and can lead to mental illness, self harm and suicide.

In many cases, the only way young people at risk of a forced marriage – usually teenage girls – can escape is by running away. This can lead to other problems such as homelessness, poverty and dropping out of education as well as increasing the risk of violence from strangers.

■ *Physical violence*

In the lead-up to a forced marriage, substantial physical violence may be used to coerce the victim into accepting the marriage.

Physical abuse to enforce a marriage can be perpetrated by almost any family member. Before the marriage, it is most often perpetrated by the victim's parents, siblings and extended family, such as uncles and cousins. Shaminder Ubhi, director of Ashiana, a women's refuge in Leyton in East London, says:

"There is a whole spectrum of abuse; sometimes it is subtle emotional pressure over a period of time but sometimes we see women who have been subjected to physical violence, abducted, forced to go Pakistan and married off against their will."

Families usually carry out the violence because they believe that the marriage is in the victim's best interests. Humera Khan, the co-founder of An-Nisa Society, a women's advocacy group in Wembley, says:

"No parent either kills the child or deliberately puts their child through a forced marriage because they hate them."

A family's desire to see their child married and with children can lead them to take extreme action. Imran Rehman, 33, a support worker at Karma Nirvana refuge in Derby was kidnapped by relatives while in Pakistan visiting family in an attempt to force him to marry his cousin, says:

"I was woken up with water splashed on my face. Several men were around me; two men held my arms and others held my legs. My brother-in-law said it was time to rehabilitate me. I was mostly swearing at them; threatening them in English. But they shackled my one leg to the other with a metal bar in between and a big ball at the back so that I couldn't walk. I was kept a prisoner there for two weeks."

If women are taken abroad to be forcibly married, the risk of them suffering violence if they refuse often increases. Family members will often be less concerned about the police than in the UK and may feel that 'western' standards of behaviour no

Shaminder Ubhi, director of Ashiana, a women's refuge in Leyton in East London, says:

66 There is a whole spectrum of abuse; sometimes it is subtle emotional pressure over a period of time but sometimes we see women who have been subjected to physical violence, abducted, forced to go Pakistan and married off against their will 99

longer apply. If the woman resists plans for a forced marriage, she can be kept abroad and subjected to regular physical and emotional violence until she agrees. It can take many years for women to submit. Many eventually agree to the forced marriage in order to be allowed to return home to the UK. Zalkha Ahmed, director of Apna Haq, a women's support group, says:

Humera Khan, the co-founder of An-Nisa Society, a women's advocacy group in Wembley, says:

66 No parent either kills the child or deliberately puts their child through a forced marriage because they hate them 99

"I am a first generation Asian, and a lot of the women who disappeared when I was growing up are slowly returning with families and that is after years of being in Pakistan. God knows what happened to the rest."

The government has not released any estimates on how many women holding British passports have been forcibly taken abroad by their relatives and not allowed to return.

■ *Psychological and emotional violence*

Emotional and psychological abuse includes a range of non-violent, psychological abuse that cause emotional damage and undermine a person's sense of well-being and self-esteem.

Women are often subjected to emotional blackmail by their relatives in the lead-up to forced marriage. Philip Balmforth, vulnerable persons' officer (Asian women) for the Bradford Police, says:

"In the 395 cases that I had [this year] there has been emotional blackmail and coercion; like pretending the mother is dying."

This form of abuse usually involves telling someone they are worthless, they will never find love and that they will bring dishonour and shame on themselves and the whole family. Other methods can include undermining a person's self-belief or telling them that the abuse will stop as soon as they are married. In some cases, women have been told that they are possessed by jinn (spirits) and that they can only be cured by visiting a holy man. Shahien Taj, the director of the Henna Foundation, a woman's refuge in Cardiff, says:

"I have come across cases where women are suffering from mental illness and are treated for being possessed by jinn. What they usually do, is that the family take them to a 'Qari' [spiritual healer] ... what he does is take a significant amount of money from certain sectors of the community. He absolutely convinces them that he has the powers to address matters of mental health. He has sessions with them like burning candles, burning paper and holding prayers – and encourages people to do the same thing."

Such practices can have severe long-term consequences. Humera Khan, co-founder of An-Nisa Society in Wembley in West London, says:

> "This leads to long term mental damage if the person is not treated by a doctor; Jinn, by definition, is something that is unknown or you can't see; it is an unknown thing. So the unknown makes people afraid."

This can, in turn, increase the chances of women suffering from depression and other emotional problems.

■ *Isolation, imprisonment and withdrawal from school*

Many families believe that if their daughters become educated, men from the same ethnic or religious group, especially those brought up abroad, will become less willing to marry them. This fear of being unable to marry off their daughters can lead parents to withdraw their children from school when they approach a marriageable age.

When girls are withdrawn from school, teachers are often reluctant to investigate for fear of being accused of racism or of stigmatising minorities. Rahni Binjie, the project manager of Roshni Asian Women's Aid, a refuge in Nottingham, says:

> "There are periods towards the end of the education process when women are taken out of school. The girls just stop coming to classes and the schools don't seem interested in following it up ... We've had women who have disappeared from the education system – and who then disappear from the system as a whole. We don't know if they've been taken abroad or killed or anything – we've got no idea."

Manjit Kaur, a women's development officer at Roshni refuge in Birmingham, was not allowed to continue her education and was sent to Pakistan to marry. She says:

> "My dad refused to send me to school and sent me to Pakistan for four years when I was younger because he believed girls should not be educated."

As a result of being withdrawn from education, women may find themselves increasingly isolated from their community and rarely allowed to leave the family home. Women can be prevented from using the phone or the internet, having visitors or seeing certain friends and family members. This also applies to well-off families who can often stand to gain money and property by marrying their daughters to another equally prosperous family.

Rahni Binjie, the project manager of Roshni Asian Women's Aid, a refuge in Nottingham, says:

66 There are periods towards the end of the education process when women are taken out of school. The girls just stop coming to classes and the schools don't seem interested in following it up 99

Philip Balmforth, vulnerable persons' officer (Asian women) for the police in Bradford, says:

Jas, a Sikh graduate, currently living in London, was subjected to intense psychological pressure by her family to force her to marry. She says:

66 Intimidation and emotional blackmail — to me — is worse than physically hitting someone. If they beat me then I would have bruises and get over it but this constant emotional blackmail destroys you from the inside out 99

"These girls are brought up to be told to do things and not ask for things; 'be the good daughter, the good wife and the good mother'. A lot of the girls are always told what to do; they are never given the choice to make a decision. I had a case where a woman who is 29 and born here is not allowed to leave the home and is imprisoned because she refused to marry their choice of husband. And as punishment she was imprisoned."

Withdrawal from school can have severe consequences for the education levels of women and can also affect their chances of gaining employment and achieving economic independence in later life (See FACTBOX: *The effect of honour on education levels*). Although the government's Forced Marriage Unit has produced guidelines for teachers on forced marriage,9 there is no obligation for teachers to take action in cases of forced marriage or even to read the guidelines.

The effect of honour on education levels

A 2007 study by the Joseph Rowntree Foundation found that the educational qualifications of women from South Asia varied widely. These variations are largely a result of their widely differing attitudes to honour.

Percentage of women aged 25-29 with degree level qualifications:

Women of Indian origin	53.9%
Women of Pakistani origin	25.6
Women of Bangladeshi origin	15.5
UK average:	29.7

Source: http://www.jrf.org.uk/bookshop/eBooks/1997-education-ethnicity-poverty.pdf p. 11. Nb. This information was based on the 2001 census

---

■ *Kidnapping and being forced to travel abroad*

Many women and some young men are tricked or blackmailed into travelling abroad and then forced into a marriage. Once in their country of origin they are often unable to refuse their family's demands.

'Saamiya', a 16-year old of Pakistani origin from the Midlands

---

9 In 2005, the Foreign and Commonwealth Office published *Dealing with Cases of Forced Marriage (1st Edition): Guidance for Education Professionals.* http://www.fco.gov.uk/Files/kfile/Dealing%20with%20cases%20of%20Forced%20Marriages.pdf

who is presently living in a refuge and who wishes to remain anonymous, says:

> "I was taken to Pakistan for a forced marriage when I was 16. My parents found out that I had a boyfriend so I was taken to Pakistan. On the 20th July I got there; and on the 21st I was told I would get married. I was told of the arranged marriage two hours before the ceremony."

The Foreign and Commonwealth Office has recorded cases where children as young as 11 have been taken back to the parents' country of origin and forced to marry.[10] There is additional evidence of other underage marriages occurring. Philip Balmforth, vulnerable persons' officer (Asian women) for the Bradford police, says:

> "I had a case of a 14 year old girl at school. The teacher tells me that the girl claims to have been married. So I went along to the school … [With a] Muslim colleague, we saw the girl. We asked her a few questions, and we were not sure, then the girl said 'if you don't believe me I have the video at home'. So in the following morning at 8:30 am we picked up the video and the pictures, made copies of them and returned them in time before school has ended. We sat down to watch, and there it was a full wedding video with the ceremony and party, it was not made up. So we had to report it to social services."

Similar situations can arise in other communities. Fathiya Yusuf, Somali community outreach worker for Refuge's office in Deptford in South London, says:

> "For many families the problem with many Somali kids is that they were born here or they came here when they were young and that as a result they become 'westernised'. Many times the family doesn't like it and so they take them back to Somalia – even though it is a war there. They take them – especially when they are teenagers – there for a holiday; for 'cultural awareness' we call it. I have noticed that sometimes they come back and they are married. I don't know if they have been made to get married or if they have fallen in love with someone there. It's not technically forced and it only happens to some people – to the 'naughty ones' as they are all it – and other people are allowed to choose to marry who they want."

Women are often told that violence and abuse will end if they agree to a marriage. In many cases, however, violence, emotional abuse and intimidation continue after even after the marriage.

'Ayesha', a Pakistani woman from northern England, says:

❝ I was raped; I didn't want to have sex with him. He was the opposite of what I was. He was twice the size of me. And anyway they would not have let me return until I got pregnant anyway. I didn't know him or meet him before and he was not related to me, he was just from the right caste ❞

---

10 On one occasion, in 2007, the Foreign and Commonwealth Office's Forced Marriage Unit reportedly rescued an 11-year old British citizen from a forced marriage in Bangladesh. *BBC*: 'Girl, 11, rescued from marriage' 8 May 2007. http://news.bbc.co.uk/1/hi/uk/6635191.stm

Abuses after a forced marriage

Some specialised refuges for South Asian women say that almost half of their service users come to them after being forced to marry. Often they have suffered various forms of domestic violence as well as marital rape, imprisonment and, in the most extreme cases, forced prostitution.

Prior to getting married, many women from honour-based cultures can face a range of restrictions on their dress, behaviour and lifestyle designed to minimise the risks of them damaging their family's honour or committing acts which will impede their chances of getting married. After being forced to marry, women can face fresh forms of abuse not only from their extended family.

■ *Rape*

Once they are forced marriage, women are sometimes raped in order to become pregnant. The rape is often condoned by the woman's parents who fear that if she does not become pregnant or have a child, she will run away.

Families from traditionalist backgrounds believe that their honour is not satisfied – and the marriage contract fulfilled – until the daughter is pregnant. If the woman fails to become pregnant or refuses to have sex, her family's honour will be damaged. 'Ayesha', a Pakistani woman from northern England, who wishes to remain anonymous for security reasons, says:

> "I was raped; I didn't want to have sex with him. He was the opposite of what I was. He was twice the size of me. And anyway they would not have let me return until I got pregnant anyway. I didn't know him or meet him before and he was not related to me, he was just from the right caste."

If the marriage takes place abroad, a family may not allow the woman to return to the UK until she has given birth in case she terminates her pregnancy on her return. 'Latifa', a 19-year old of Pakistani origin who fled to a refuge to escape a forced marriage, says:

> "The guy I was supposed to get married to was my aunty's son. And because I didn't get married to him, they gave him my sister instead. That's what it's like. She's in Pakistan now. She's 16 and she's pregnant. They had promised me verbally to him and his family when I was born. But now because I've run away they've given my sister to him instead. My sister blames me because she's in this situation – she's

three months pregnant and has been married for four months. My dad won't bring her back till she's had the baby."

Even in the UK, marital rape is common in some cases. Shahien Taj, the director of the Henna Foundation, a women's group in Cardiff says:

"What we find is that women [from abroad] accept physical commitment from their partners during marriage, because they just don't know that they can say no. This goes for imported brides and people from here. With brides that were brought up here, when they find out what has happened, they are actually traumatised about it."

In some cases, rape can also take the form of prostitution. On a few occasions, families have reportedly married their children from abroad in order to import a bride to work in prostitution. Sana Bukhari, an outreach worker at Ashiana in Sheffield, says:

"I have one case when someone was brought over and her husband had mental health issues; he had the mental age of a five year old but the body of a 40 year old. It was a telephone nikah, so the girl only saw what he looked like on picture and thought 'gosh he looks good'. When she finally arrived she found out that he was disabled, and this girl was very pretty, so the mother in law decided to invite all these men over, and it was prostitution. The girl however managed to escape and go to the police."

The police have encountered similar practices. Philip Balmforth, vulnerable persons' officer (Asian women) for the Bradford police force, says:

"There have been a lot of enquiries made in the Keighley area after work done by Ann Cryer [MP for Keighley], but we have come across cases there. I have heard from other people that imported brides can be sometimes used for prostitution ... I just had a call this morning from the housing office about two girls, aged 16 who have gone missing from the refuge, these two Asian girls were groomed for prostitution, so I passed that on to the missing person's officer."

In Keighley, such abuses are well-known and documented thanks to the campaigning work done by Ann Cryer the local MP. In other parts of the UK, MPs are more reluctant to get involved in such controversial issues.

■ *Abandonment*

Women's groups report that an increasing number of women brought from South Asia to marry British men are being referred to the voluntary sector and social services after their husbands abandoned them in the UK. On many occasions they are not entitled to benefits, hold few qualifications and cannot speak English fluently.

Women who are abandoned by their husbands can be left destitute and may be rejected or subjected to violence from their own relatives who believe they have damaged their family's honour.

C A S E   S T U D Y

ABUSE FROM IN-LAWS AFTER A FORCED MARRIAGE

Rukhsana, now 23, was forced to marry when she was 18. After her marriage she was abused by her husband and in-laws. She doesn't speak English.

I didn't know my husband personally – he chose me but I didn't choose him. It wasn't a choice; you don't say 'no'; you marry who your parents tell you. But his mother didn't approve of his choice and she always told me so – she wanted him to marry his cousin.

The violence started four months into the pregnancy in 2003, a year after the marriage. I suffered violence from him and the family over domestic issues. The women in his family would beat me and they turned him against me.

They hit me while pregnant and that included kicking and punching. It could be by not doing chores around the house, if I used the phone without their permission or if I tried to leave the house.

I received very poor medical care after the baby was delivered. Every time a health worker came to check on the baby, they would pretend that everything was normal and then resume to beat me and humiliate me in front of my husband. They clearly didn't want me; they believed that I was not worthy enough to marry into their family. My mother-in-law degraded me on many occasion and used to instigate violence against me.

They didn't categorically say that I could not go out, but they never took me out, and they refused me any telephone access. My mother died and I didn't know till months after because they didn't tell me and I couldn't contact my family in Pakistan. That hurt me deeply, I loved my mother, and they deprived me from my basic human rights.

The last straw was when I was late preparing breakfast for my mother-in-law as I was seeing to my child as she had been crying all morning. My husband came in and started verbally abusing me because I was late with the breakfast. I thought nothing of it because it was just another morning, so then I took my girl to school and when I returned it was blown into a full argument.

[The mother, husband and sister then set up on her. They attacked her, punching, kicking and hitting her with blunt kitchen objects.]

I was left with multiple wounds, bruises and fractures. I retreated to the room demoralised and suicidal. But I couldn't kill myself as I thought about my daughter and what kind of life she would have without her mother because they never treated her right and just ignored her, calling her names and treating her like an outcast.

When the coast was clear, I escaped, and went to her school and asked for help while collecting my daughter in the process. I knew that there was no turning back after that humiliating beating.

23

Sana Bukhari, an outreach worker for Ashiana, a women's refuge in Sheffield, explains:

> "When they bring someone here to marry, they do it for the sake of the family. But when she is here they are hit with the reality that person is here to stay, and that they don't really like them. I had one case in Liverpool yesterday that lasted 12 hours, because they wanted to deport this woman. Her marriage lasted one week, she arrived here and found that her husband had already been married twice and has children and didn't tell her or her family. Within a week she left because he beat her immediately. Even though her family know that he has beaten her, lied about not being married and having other kids, they said 'don't you dare come back here'. They are not bothered about her, just about the dishonour of leaving the relationship."

In these situations, the pressure lies solely on the woman who is seen as responsible for upholding her family's honour. There is often no comparable shame attached to the husband's family for ending the marriage or abandoning his wife. Zalkha Ahmed, the director of Apna Haq, a women's group, says:

> "There is no pressure on a man; look at forced marriage – once that marriage is done, the man can escape easily; the women do all the house work and the man usually has a girlfriend on the side; it is still to a man's advantage. There are certain situations when men have had no choice, but that's few. A man can get a divorce; a woman can't. And if a woman leaves the marriage, no one is going to touch her."

On many occasions husbands have "dumped" their imported brides and returned to their native country to remarry, sometimes as many as four to five times.

■ Depression, self harm and suicide resulting from forced marriages

Many women forced into marriage have so deeply internalised concepts of honour that they may feel unable to defy their families. In consequence, women being forced into a marriage who suffer violence and abuse often suffer depression, anxiety and other psychological problems that can lead to self-harm, schizophrenia and suicide.

In many cases, the contradiction between how women are told to act by their families and the personal freedoms which they see enjoyed by wider society can create complex psychological problems. Rania Hafez, principle lecturer in Education at the University of East London, says:

Rania Hafez, principle lecturer in Education at the University of East London, says:

66 What you have in Britain is a multicultural society where the norms and values learnt at home are not corresponding to the norms and values learned outside. The child who goes out has a contradiction and a conflict – it's about managing the conflict 99

C A S E   S T U D Y

SIKH VICTIM OF SERIAL ARRANGED MARRIAGES

Raj, a Sikh girl from the Midlands, was married at the age of twenty-two in 2002. She is a Sikh from the Punjab region of India. Her husband was 35. She does not speak English.

I only met him once before the marriage and agreed straight away because that is the norm, you don't really have a say when your parents chose someone for you. My parents responded to an advert in the newspaper. The advert said: 'Guy from England is seeking a girl [from] this town, must be Sikh, nice family etc...'

He lied on the advert because he said he was an engineer, but he was a builder living at home in the West Midlands with his family; the description was a lie, both me and my family where deceived. He was the same caste as me: Ramgharia.

We had a Gurdwara Sikh wedding in India, and once I arrived in the UK, there was no civil marriage. I was always brought up to think that I was going to get an arranged marriage in that form, also [that it was part of] my role in the family and the community. That's the school of thought; you get forced into a marriage where there is no love. He was also forced into it; but, it is easier for him.

Once I moved to England I was not allowed any contact with the family or my other sister in England. I had no contact with anyone. All I ever did was the cooking and cleaning and try to make children. That was all there was in my life. I only got sixty pounds in five years from him. I had to beg for money and things and I was made to feel [like] a servant. I had to beg for them to sort out my immigration permit, and it was done reluctantly.

He was previously divorced because his first wife did not have any children, and he married me so that I [could] have children; when I didn't have any children the problem just got worse, and I was blamed for the situation.

After a year I was forced to receive IVF treatment at the hospital. I was given fertility drugs and fertility treatment from a relative [who was a] family doctor. It was forced [on me] by him and his family, but I think the problem was him and not me.

Compared to other relationships you see in the refuge, mine wasn't severe in terms of physical abuse; it was all psychological. I didn't have contact with him, apart from the odd occasion when we had sex, and I stayed this long so that I won't bring shame to my family.

I think that there should be some sort of punishment or restrictions on people going to another country to marry for the second or the third time. Also when someone arrives here there should be some sort of monitoring programme to insure the girl is safe.

If the person gets divorced for the second time with a marriage from abroad then the government should intervene to see what is exactly going wrong for someone to have to marry for the second or third time from abroad.

"What you have in Britain is a multicultural society where the norms and values learnt at home are not corresponding to the norms and values learned outside. The child who goes out has a contradiction and a conflict – it's about managing the conflict."

It is a conflict which many women are unable to resolve. Jatinder

Chana, project worker at Asha Projects, a refuge in Streatham in South London, says:

> "The majority of women [who we see] have mental health needs. Anxiety, depression and self harm are a huge issue with young girls."

'Ayesha', a Pakistani woman now working at a women's refuge in northern England, who attempted suicide when she discovered her parents were planning to send her to Pakistan to be married, says:

> "I found out here that they were going to take me abroad and marry me off, so I thought if I took a massive overdose they would have to take me to the hospital and I won't have to go. So I took the overdose thinking that it would get me into hospital and from there I could ask for help — somewhere, somehow I had to get out of the house. So in the end I took the overdose and within hours I was puking blood everywhere. They didn't care, I pleaded with them to take me to the hospital and they were like 'you are still getting on that plane and there is nothing you can do about it'."

Often such situations are made worse because young women are unable to turn to family members for help while also being prevented from meeting friends. Sana Bukhari, project worker at Ashiana, woman's refuge in Sheffield, says:

> "Isolation is the biggest problem [Asian women] face and they have to get used to it because they can't turn to the male family members."

There are no recent statistics on the rates of suicide and self-harm among South Asian women in the UK. For example, the widely cited figure that South Asian women are "three-times more likely" to commit suicide than white women dates from 1992.[11] Some recent reports suggest that this figure may have increased. For example, in 2007, First Great Western train service reported that during 2006, 80 people had committed suicide by jumping onto train tracks between Paddington and Slough.[12] Women's groups from London have said that they believe that a disproportionately large number of these were Asian women.[13]

'Rukhsana', 23, was forced into a marriage in Pakistan at 18 before being brought to the UK. Abused by her British husband and in-laws, she ran away from home with her daughter. She says:

> ❝ I couldn't kill myself as I thought about my daughter and what kind of life she would have without her mother because they never treated her right and just ignored her, calling her names and treating her like an outcast. No one could ever understand what I am going through — depression, anxiety and not being able to think straight. I feel helpless and hopeless; there is nothing to keep me going on living apart from my daughter ❞

---

11 Raleigh, V.S. & Balarajan, R. 1992, 'Suicide and Self-Burning among Indians and West Indians in England and Wales', *British Journal of Psychiatry*, 129, 365-368. http://www.mind.org.uk/Information/Factsheets/Suicide/#_ftn24

12 *Daily Mail*: 'Abused' Asian women behind soaring toll of railway suicides, by Glen Owen and Oliver Wadsen. 22nd September 2007.
http://www.dailymail.co.uk/pages/live/articles/news/news.html?in_article_id=483315&in_page_id=1770

13 *Daily Mail*: 'Abused' Asian women behind soaring toll of railway suicides, by Glen Owen and Oliver Wadsen. 22nd September 2007.
http://www.dailymail.co.uk/pages/live/articles/news/news.html?in_article_id=483315&in_page_id=1770

CHAPTER 3

Honour-based domestic violence

Introduction

The Home Office defines domestic violence as "any incident of threatening behaviour, violence or abuse between adults who are or have been in a relationship together, or between family members, regardless of gender or sexuality".[14]Some government departments and voluntary agencies use slightly broader definitions which acknowledge the possibility of violence from relatives. The definition used by the Association of Chief Police Office (ACPO), for instance, is "threatening behaviour, violence or abuse (psychological, physical, sexual, financial or emotional) between adults (aged 18 or over) who are or have been intimate partners or are family members, regardless of gender or sexuality".[15]

Honour-based domestic violence differs significantly from more common forms of domestic violence since it can also be carried out by a person's children, siblings, in-laws and extended family. Although honour-based violence is frequently related to forced marriage, such abuse often aims to more generally protect the family's reputation and honour from gossip and slander. Zalkha Ahmed, director of Apna Haq, a woman's refuge, says:

> "It is to stop people from talking about you, but it always seems to be loaded on the women, the man can do what he wants and no-one talks about them."

Honour-based domestic violence in general occurs because a woman's spouse, relatives or in-laws think that their family's social status is more important than the woman's individual welfare. Sana Bukhari, outreach worker at Ashiana, a woman's group in Sheffield, says:

> "Honour to them is all about appearance and how they look on the

❝ You know some people still don't understand that their husbands can't hit them, and that that is called domestic violence. They don't even know what it is ❞

Abigail Morris, director of Jewish Women's Aid in London

---

14 Home Office website: *Domestic violence: What is meant by domestic violence?* http://www.homeoffice.gov.uk/crime-victims/reducing-crime/domestic-violence/

15 See for example, *ACPO Guidance: Identifying, Assessing and Managing Risk in the context of Policing Domestic Violence* (ACPO, February 2005)p. 9 http://www.acpo.police.uk/asp/policies/Data/250205DV%20Risk%20Assessment%20(ACPO%20Draft%20Guidance15.3%20last).doc

surface and they have to be the perfect family otherwise the community looks down on them and does not accept them; to them the community comes first. It is living for others and not living for yourself and it is more important than the life of the daughter."

In this context, violence (when not related to forced marriage) can be provoked by acting 'western', defying the wishes of one's parents, families and in-laws, or being sexually independent. As in all communities such domestic violence can also be exacerbated by drug and alcohol abuse and stress (related, for instance, to poverty and unemployment) on the part of the perpetrator and/or the victim.

Forms of honour-based domestic violence

■ *Defying parental authority*

Women often suffer psychological abuse and physical violence from their relatives if they are seen as defying parental authority or acting in a 'western' manner which could damage the family's reputation and their standing in the local community.

Emotional and physical violence are often used by families and spouses to ensure that women conform to their community's traditions and cultural norms. Such violence is also used to punish women for actions or behaviour which the community may consider 'unacceptable'. Shaminder Ubhi, director of Ashiana in Leyton in East London says:

> "Parents and families often use a range of abuses that can be emotional and physical to stop or prevent their children from behaving in a way that they see as unacceptable and that happens a lot."

Psychological and emotional abuse can also play an important role in controlling and punishing women. This can involve withholding money, confining the person in their room or house to separate them from the outside world and their friends and removing them from education. Jas, a Sikh graduate from Birmingham, has experienced most of the psychological violence mentioned above. She says:

> "Intimidation and emotional blackmail to me is worse than physical violence, because it has long term effects. I would get ignored at family functions. I would not even get invited to my brother's birthday. They would all go out while I was left at home."

66 Domestic violence is a huge problem. I'd say 60 per cent of Arab families suffer from domestic violence. The main problem is the lack of awareness within the community on the violence and its effects 99

Mohamed Baleela, project worker at the Domestic Violence Intervention Project in West London

C A S E   S T U D Y

ARRANGED MARRIAGE AND FLEEING TO A REFUGE

Haley is an Orthodox Jewish woman. After having an arranged marriage she suffered domestic violence from her husband. She escaped to live in a refuge for Jewish women. She now works in a women's refuge part-time:

Mine wasn't an arranged marriage, but that happens in the Jewish community; it's quite prominent. Women in arranged marriages can't leave the marriage because then the family is soiled; it's family and pride. So they tend to live with the domestic violence for the sake of the family. There are plenty of happy arranged marriages.

I lived in a refuge, 2003-4. I came through the help of the police who referred me to the refuge. And I didn't mention that I was Jewish because you just don't know if there is anything available. So I went into a Hertfordshire refuge with women of all backgrounds; a complete cross culture.

I couldn't eat in the house, cook in the kitchen, I couldn't observe the Sabbath. I was completely cut off, so the few weeks later during [the] Christmas period, I found on the internet that a Jewish women's refuge existed, so I moved into it during New Years Eve.

My husband chased after and was after me. I was mainly worried about my two year old daughter, who was in the refuge with me. At the time she was at an orthodox nursery. And my life then was thrown up in the air; I didn't want to disturb her while she was going to nursery school.

I couldn't turn to my family because they live away by the coast; they are retired and living in a non -Jewish neighbourhood. And that's it, that's all I have in the UK.

Once I came to the refuge, the women there: two were extremely orthodox, with children and covered hair. Some were secular but able to understand, and some were like myself, United [secular and orthodox] but not orthodox. I am orthodox, as in I keep the Sabbath, but I don't cover my head. I was able to fit with all the women there.

The backgrounds they came from, before they ran from abusive husbands, were similar. They didn't know that they weren't supposed to be treated like that, with the Orthodox women. They thought it was part and parcel of married life.

I was very lucky with my experience, I was only in the refuge for six months, however during that period I was declared bankrupt, I lost my house, all my possessions and my job. My daughter did get into a Jewish school, which is fine. I was then re-housed in a housing association house.

Now I volunteer here part-time because I just want to help. You will find a lot of that with the volunteers, a lot of them used the service and have returned to help.

In the Kurdish community, male members of the family are usually seen as the guardian of cultural norms and values. If a woman contravenes those norms and values, the male guardian is often obliged to act to protect the community's belief system. Gona Saed, director of the Middle East Centre for Woman's Rights, an advocacy group in South London, says:

> "It's a combination of nationalistic traditions, culture and religion. These all feed into this violence against women."

29

In such contexts, physical violence can be carried by almost any member of the family. Fathers, brothers, and mothers can all feel that they have the right to use violence to control their female relatives' behaviour. Shaminder Ubhi, director of Ashiana, a woman's refuge in Leyton in South East London, says:

> "We have cases when it is not the mother and father that are abusing their children, it is sometimes the extended family members. It does not only happen abroad; it happens here. This could take the form of emotional and physical abuse; sometimes sexual abuse where they could be raped. On these occasion it is not the parents that are playing the central role; it is the extended family that could start with brothers."

Activists in the Arab community believe that honour-based domestic violence often occurs if a woman defies the authority of her husband, brother or parent. Mohamed Baleela, project worker at the Domestic Violence intervention Project in Hammersmith in West London, says:

> "Domestic violence is a huge problem. I'd say 60 per cent of Arab families suffer from domestic violence. The main problem is the lack of awareness within the community on the violence and its affects. It is a huge stigma because it is associated with shame. An Arabic-speaking woman would not want to be seen as breaking up her family. Community leaders and imams see keeping the family together as much more important."

Patterns of violence in the Jewish community can be similar to those of more recent immigrants – even though many Jewish families have lived in the UK for centuries. As in South Asian and Middle Eastern cultures, many Jews from conservative backgrounds can may see women as the upholders of family and community values and put a high premium on traditional family values. In addition, Jewish women are often seen as being the carriers of their community's religious identity. As in other communities, however, this can become a pretext for violence and abuse. Abigail Morris, director of Jewish Women's Aid in North London, says:

> "There is something called 'Shalom bait', that says you must have peace in your house; some women who go forward to the rabbi and tell them that they have a problem, they get told to go back to their homes and make peace – as if it's their responsibility rather than the rabbi acknowledging that there is a problem with the husband. They say stuff like 'go home make peace ... cook a nice dinner ... wait in for him.'"

Mohamed Baleela, project worker at the Domestic Violence intervention Project in Hammersmith in West London, says:

66 Domestic violence is a huge problem. I'd say 60 per cent of Arab families suffer from domestic violence. The main problem is the lack of awareness within the community on the violence and its affects 99

As in other communities, violence in Jewish groups can take many forms. In some cases, Jewish men have hit their partners with religious objects. Haley, a volunteer outreach worker with Jewish Women's Aid who is herself a victim of honour-based violence, says:

"We had a woman who was hit over the head with a large set basin, [which is used in the ritual of netilat yadayim, the washing of the hands before meals]. She never knew that her husband can't hit her, she thought it was normal. And this was a religious ornament, a sacred jug to wash her hand. Now she will have to see this thing every time she is ready to eat, it will traumatise her."

The Jewish experience shows that even members of the most prosperous and long-established immigrant groups in the UK can preserve their traditional honour-based value systems for centuries despite being exposed to a range of competing ideas and value-systems.

Some women's groups say that ideas that family members should physically punish female relatives who damage their family's honour are also found in some white British communities. Rahni Binjie, the project manager of Roshni Women's Aid, a refuge in Nottingham, says:

"In some cases we don't see that there is a lot of difference [between white and Asian families]. If you go to some of the white working class communities up North you still can find this strong sense of community and the feeling of being part of a large extended family."

■ Acting 'western'

Honour-based violence is often initiated against women who are seen to be acting too 'western' or who have relationships or friendships which transgress gender, caste, ethnic or religious distinctions.

Women's behaviour which is viewed as 'unacceptable' by families and communities can include having a boyfriend of different race, religion, caste or wearing 'western' style clothing and listening to 'western' music. Sana Bukhari, outreach worker at Ashiana, a women's refuge in Sheffield, says:

"Honour is about stopping people talking, anything different is seen as deviant and not acceptable – as it is not the norm. The family didn't want to be seen as different. And the norm is what people want to reach and achieve, it is the moral code in to which you live your life."

Rahni Binjie, the project manager of Roshni Women's Aid, a refuge in Nottingham, says:

66 In some cases we don't see that there is a lot of difference [between white and Asian families]. If you go to some of the white working class communities up North you still can find this strong sense of community and the feeling of being part of a large extended family 99

Shahien Taj, director of the Henna Foundation, a women's group in Cardiff, says that members of the city's Muslim community, one of the UK's longest established Islamic communities, have distributed circulars that 'name and shame' women who are seen acting too 'western'. Some of these detailed newsletters (See *Appendix*) have, she says, been sent to almost 1,250 Muslim homes with the aim of publicising the 'immoral' behaviour of certain individuals – mainly women – and calling on the community to take action against them. She says:

> "These circulars name and shame people that break the honour codes of the community. These circulars are highly damaging to the individuals mentioned in them. The circulars are there to enforce the power and control of the community leaders in an attempt to police their community. This also could lead the family to use violence to control their daughters and this has happened, with many women mentioned previously going into hiding."

Families seen as unable to control their daughters can themselves be ostracised and described as a "loose family" by members of their community. Mohamed Baleela, project worker for Domestic Violence Intervention Project in Hammersmith in West London, says:

> "Whispers will go around and they will be talking behind the family's back about honour, the girls' virginity, whether she has a boyfriend or not. It also affects them back home because the word will spread and the family name will be tainted. We have had people who have decided to leave Britain because they fear for their daughter's honour. It's a big, big issue for a lot of families."

It is partly fear of such social ostracism which can drive parents to use violence against their own children. In some communities, even seemingly straightforward acts such as allowing women to go to university can be viewed as immoral and 'western' in such circumstances. Extreme pressures can be put on women to drop out of education. Jas, a Sikh woman from Birmingham, says:

> "My family were suffocating me with pressure and making me guilty for going to university because of what people were saying. My mother would cry all the time, my father would say things like I am bringing shame to the family by not leaving university and coming back to marry; and how difficult it has become for him to show his face around. In the eyes of the community, by going to the university I was seen as a 'girl gone wild'."

Premarital relationships are taboo in most South Asian and Middle Eastern society. Most premarital relationships in these com-

Bawjit Singh, an Indian Hindu who works as a social worker in East London whose sister was disowned by her family after marrying a Muslim, says:

66 In the eyes of my parents marrying a Muslim is marrying the enemy. We are taught that we can be friends with them but we can't date them and definitely can't marry them. If I marry one who is Muslim then I am disowned 99

munities are conducted in secret. This is especially true when relationships cut across racial or religious boundaries. Bawjit Singh, an Indian Hindu who works as a social worker in East London whose sister was disowned by her family after marrying a Muslim, says:

> "In the eyes of my parents marrying a Muslim is marrying the enemy. We are taught that we can be friends with them but we can't date them and definitely can't marry them. If I marry one who is Muslim then I am disowned."

Such relationships can trigger extreme violence between families. Philip Balmforth, the vulnerable person's officer (Asian women) for Bradford's police force, says:

> "There are so many incidents when families have turned violent on other families for the reason of kids running away together. One case even included a shot gun being fired at a family's house."

In many instances, the police and local authorities wrongly categorise such attacks as being racially – or religiously – motivated. Such errors can lead to the prevalence of honour-based violence being underestimated.

■ *Control by in-laws*

The majority of women's refuges report that many of their clients have suffered abuse from their in-laws who seek to control women who have married into their family. In many cases, this situation is exacerbated because many South Asian customs often require newly married couples to live in their husbands' family home.

On many occasions, as soon as the women has are married they are subjected to psychological abuse, followed by violence if the person continues to step out of line. 'Sakina', a Pakistani woman currently in a West Midlands women's refuge, says:

> "[My mother in-law] started hitting me and then pushed me down the stairs. I was semi-unconscious, but that didn't stop her with hitting me around the head with her shoes till I completely passed out. I can't remember the amount of times I have been abused; it was a daily thing with my husband, his mother and sister getting involved. Sometimes I had an iron thrown at me but not by my husband, he only used to punch and kick me."

As a means of control, families often restrict the victim's day-to-day activities and limit their contact with the outside world. Raj,

Philip Balmforth, the vulnerable person's officer (Asian women) for Bradford's police force, says:

❝ There are so many incidents when families have turned violent on other families for the reason of kids running away together. One case even included a shot gun being fired at a family's house ❞

a Sikh woman currently living in a women's refuge in the West Midlands after escaping a violent forced marriage, says:

> "Once I moved to England I was not allowed to have any contact with the family or my other sister in England. I had no contact with anyone. I never left home during the marriage. They only place I have been to was the garden. I did think that this was normal because it is similar to Pakistan, but sometimes there you are allowed to leave. The only time I tried to leave the house my mother in-law pulled my hair. I think I only wanted to go out and help fetch something."

Support groups say that many women simply do not understand the concept of domestic violence. Manjit Kaur, a development officer for Roshni, a women's refuge in Birmingham, says:

> "We have checked other languages, like Hindi and Gujarati, and still there was no words used to describe domestic violence. Ask a woman if she is suffering domestic violence, they think it is physical but it is also mental, and they don't know; we are working on a word, but we haven't found one yet."

Many women feel unable to leave such abusive situations because they are themselves bound by notions of honour and shame. Many believe that if they leave they will bring shame on to their family and on themselves.

■ Drug and alcohol abuse

Drug and alcohol abuse causes increased violence against women within ethnic and religious communities – just as it does among other communities. In some cases, a belief among immigrant communities that drug and alcohol issues are 'western' problems or are somehow 'deserved' can make it harder for victims and perpetrators to seek help and treatment.

In Muslim communities, in particular, there is often a lack of support and understanding for drug and alcohol addicts. Zahia Tatimahand, director of Kiran Asian Women's Aid, a refuge in Leytonstone in East London, says:

> "It does not matter which community people come from, there are still drugs and alcohol in Muslim communities. The problem is more so for Muslims, because if you are not meant to be drinking, who do you turn to when you have a problem?"

Seeking treatment or admitting to such problems can also be seen as shameful for oneself and one's family. Ila Patel, director of the Asha Project, a refuge in Streatham in South London, says:

Nicola Sharp, policy manager at Refuge in central London, says:

66 We don't see poverty or economic deprivation as a direct cause of domestic violence because we believe that violence is a choice that people make. But we do recognise that these factors might contribute to situations which can lead to violence – through causing arguments for instance 99

"We have dealt with cases of domestic violence through drug and alcohol abuse, but what we would say is that while there is honour attached to leaving the family, there is also honour involved in disclosing that there are substance abuse issues."

Fear of such shame can discourage Muslim drug and alcohol addicts from seeking help or treatment. This can help perpetuate domestic violence.

■ Economic factors

Stresses caused by unemployment can also fuel honour-based domestic violence. Women's groups, however, say that poverty in itself is very rarely a direct cause of violence.

Nicola Sharp, policy manager at Refuge in central London, says:

"We don't see poverty or economic deprivation as a direct cause of domestic violence because we believe that violence is a choice that people make. But we do recognise that these factors might contribute to situations which can lead to violence – through causing arguments for instance."

In many communities of immigrant origin, rates of unemployment are often far above the national average (*see* FACTBOX *below*). This can lead to socio-economic deprivation as well as increasing the feelings of inadequacy and frustration which can often drive men to abuse women. Stresses related to unemployment and lack of money can be further compounded by language and economic barriers. Rania Hafez, principle lecturer in education at the University of East London, says:

Economic activity among Britain's immigrants

Percentage rates of employment, unemployment and economic inactivity (i.e. persons not available for work and/or not actively seeking work) for working age population by country of birth in 2005/6.

	Employed	Unemployed	Economically inactive
Indians	71%	4%	25%
Pakistanis	45%	55%	50%
Bangladeshis	44%	8%	48%
Somalis	19%	10%	71%
(UK average	78%	4%	18%)

Source: Britain's Immigrants: An Economic Profile, Institute of Public Policy Research, London, 2007. Table 6.2, page 34

"It is clear that when you face cultural differences and language barriers your chances of getting employed are reduced and men become marginalised. This could lead to a great feeling of anxiety and pressure which in turn leads to violence against the vulnerable – which is usually the wife or the daughter."

There is not always a direct correlation between lack of economic opportunity and high levels of domestic violence, however. Somalis, for example have some of the highest levels of unemployment and benefit dependency of any immigrant group in the UK. According to some estimates, 80 per cent of those born in Somalia live in social housing.[16] Despite this, however, groups working with Somalis say that the level of honour-based violence among the community is often lower than in other communities. Fathiya Yusuf, a Somali community outreach worker for Refuge in South East London, says:

"It's usually emotional or psychological abuse rather than physical. Physical domestic violence is not an issue in our community. He will not hit her but he will make her be depressed; she will be mentally abused, psychologically abused; the man will use her immigration status against her, not allow her to go out, meet friends or family. He will find ways to control her; through financial control, emotional and psychological control. Since I began working here seven years ago I have only come across four cases where people have been attacked."

Others say that honour-based violence is no more prevalent among unemployed or unskilled immigrants and may be just as high – or even higher – in richer families. Judy Morgan, director of the Lantern Project in Birmingham, says:

"I think what you will find that higher up the ladder the perpetrators are financially solvent but also the more intelligent they are, the more difficult it is for someone to get away from them, especially if they have a profession. If you have someone who is married to a judge, a barrister or a solicitor, then it is a different story; he knows the law, he has contacts."

Other workers in women's groups say that women from wealthy or 'upper class' families may feel greater shame from approaching charities, local authorities and women's refuges than women from lower-status households. This may deter them from seeking help.

---

16 'Britain's Immigrants: An Economic Profile', IPPR report fig. 5.13 (page 30)

CHAPTER 4

Honour killings

Introduction

Honour killings are the most extreme example of instances where community values and interests are imposed on individuals at the expense of their most basic human right: the right to life. The United Nations Population Fund has estimated that around 5,000 women die in honour killings every year worldwide, the vast majority in Pakistan, India and Bangladesh.[17] Such murders are usually carried out against women who act in a manner which a community (whether their immediate or extended family, co-religionists or inhabitants of their town, a district) finds unacceptable. The large-scale immigration of people from these regions and others means that such killings – of both men and women – now occur in the UK.

How many honour killings in the UK?

The police and the Crown Prosecution Service have said that on average 10-12 women are killed in honour-based violence every year in the UK.[18] If this figure is true, honour killings would amount to a relatively small proportion of the total number of murders committed annually in the UK.[19] However, the exact number of honour killings in the UK is not known – partly because there is no clear definition of what constitutes an hon-

---

17 The United Nations Population Fund: 'A Human Rights and Health Priority'. http://www.unfpa.org/swp/2000/english/ch03.html

18 The police estimate of 10-12 honour-killings a year is widely quoted by the British media. This figure seems to originate with Commander Andy Baker who said on 29th September 2003 that the police estimated that 10-12 honour killings occurred in the UK every year. He said on the day that Abdulla Yones was convicted for the murder of his daughter, Heshu. See: *The Guardian*: 'Kurd who slit daughter's throat in 'honour killing' is jailed for life' by Vikram Dodd 30 September 2003, *The Independent*: 'Execute me, pleads Muslim who killed daughter after she took western boyfriend boyfriend' by Terri Judd 30 September 2003, *Birmingham Post*: 'Women pay high price for 'shame'' 30 September 2003 and *Yorkshire Post*: ''Honour killings' claim lives of 13 women a day' 29 September 2003.

19 According to the Home Office there were 839 recorded murders in the UK between April 2004-March 2005. Home Office Statistical Bulletin, 'Warning signs and symptoms of domestic abuse, Violent Crime Overview, Homicide and Gun Crime 2004/2005' (2nd edition), by Kathryn Coleman, Celia Hird and David Povey. January 2006. Page 49. http://www.homeoffice.gov.uk/rds/pdfs06/hosb0206.pdf

our killing – and many believe the true figure could be higher[20].
Philip Balmforth, vulnerable persons' officer (Asian women) for
the Bradford police force, says:

> "From my position in Bradford, it seems that the figure [12 honour
> killings a year] could be much higher."

In particular, usually only honour-killings by those of immigrant
descent are classified as honour-killings. Workers in women's
groups say that many murders carried out by white Britons of
partners and family members are also based on ideas of honour.
Humera Khan, the co-founder of An-Nisa Society, a women's
advocacy group in Wembley in London, says:

Olivia Madden, client co-ordinator for
Panah, a refuge in Newcastle, says:

**66 We have worked with women
who were taken abroad and just
disappeared 99**

> "Just because honour issues are not associated with white people
> does not mean that it does not happen. It happens, but not in the
> way that people talk about it when it happens in a Muslims or Asian
> context. What fuels honour in Asian and Middle Eastern culture and
> the frame work lies within feudalism, tribalism and patriarchal ways
> of living. Those things do not exist within white secular families. If an
> honour killing in these communities occurs it is usually referred to as a
> "crime of passion". But underneath this, the basic drivers such as pride
> and honour are still the same even if the motives are different."

There have also been several cases where South Asian and Kurdish women have been taken abroad, "back home", and may have
been killed. Olivia Madden, client co-ordinator for Panah, a refuge in Newcastle, says:

> "We have worked with women who were taken abroad and just dis-
> appeared."

There are also no figures of the overall number of honour-related
deaths – for instance, on the number of women driven to suicide.
Tanisha Jnagel, the community services team leader for Roshni
Women's Aid, a refuge in Nottingham, says:

> "We know of a lot of women who have been scalded and who have
> died as a result of their injuries – but there's often been no adequate
> investigation to classify that as a honour killing – or even to say if it was
> an accident or if it was a murder."

---

20 It is notably that usually only honour-killings of women by men of South Asian and
Middle Eastern origin are classified as such – murders carried out for similar reasons by
white Britons or those of European, African and South American origin might not be
similarly categorised.

As a result of these factors it seems likely that the number of honour-killings is significantly higher than estimates produced by the police or the Home Office.

Honour killings among people of South Asian origin

Summary

Most of the honour killings known to have occurred in the UK appear to have been carried out be people of South Asian Origin.[21] Most of these murders are carried out by Muslims from Pakistan and Bangladesh. Hindus and Sikhs also carry out honour killings but seemingly at a proportionally lower rate. Although many – and perhaps most – honour-related murders are carried out by first-generation immigrants to the UK, an increasing number also involve people born and raised in Britain. Honour killings by South Asians occur nationwide. Although there have been several such killings in towns in the Midlands and the North, there is little evidence to suggest that such crimes are much more prevalent there than in London and the South East.

Several of the murders have been carried out by relatively well-off immigrants who would usually be regarded as "well-integrated". This suggests that lack of education or socio-economic deprivations do not, in themselves, cause honour killings. Such killings are instead often more indicative of the extent to which a family will go to defend its own traditions against ideas of female independence and freedom of thought and action which they regard as 'western' and therefore as morally and ethically inferior to their own South Asian value system. A woman's own willingness to break traditional cultural, social and religious taboos is also an important factor. If women's actions are tightly controlled and their behaviour remains within traditional norms, violence is unnecessary; families only kill when they fear that a woman freeing herself from traditional controls will damage their standing in their community. Nazir Afzal, the Crown Prosecution Service's lead on honour-based violence, says:

> "A factor that links integration and honour-crimes is that obviously women are more likely to be exposed to foreign ideas than they would be in South Asia. This leads to tensions within the community and within the family that leads to honour-based violence. The women who are trying to integrate are more likely to become victims of honour-based violence."

Raj, a 27-year old Sikh woman who is staying in a refuge in the West Midlands, fled her marital home because she feared that her in-laws were planning to kill her for failing to produce a child. She says:

❝ Although I had fertility treatment in the UK, they were going to send me to India for special treatment, but I know there was nothing wrong with me and getting treatment there could be dangerous to me; that I would probably be dumped or killed ❞

---

21 According to in-house analysis of honour-killings reported in the UK media between 1990 and 2007.

HONOUR KILLINGS IN SOUTH ASIA

South Asian: Honour killings occur across the Indian subcontinent. The killings are carried out by followers of all South Asian religions although it is usually more common among Muslims, among minorities in Muslim-majority areas and among Muslims in areas where they themselves are a minority.

Pakistan: Some studies estimate that up to a thousand women die in Pakistan every year in honour violence – although no systematic survey has been carried out.[1] A 2004 study by Oxfam estimated that 450 women in Pakistan are killed every year in honour-based violence.[2] Many women's groups in Pakistan say the number of honour killings is increasing – although there are no precise figures to support this. Several groups link the alleged rise in honour killings to the growing popularity of Islamist parties who have opposed government plans to increase sentences against those guilty of honour-killing.[3] A 2007 report by Amnesty International noted that the "practice is by no means waning".[4] Another report focusing on Pakistan's North West Frontier Province found that honour killings are carried out to punish women for even minor acts of disobedience: "What triggers honor killing is not restricted to the perceived or actual illicit sexual relation of a woman but could be any autonomous decision on the part of a woman."[5]

India: In India at least a thousand women are believed to be killed every year for honour-related reasons. Oxfam estimates that "every six hours, somewhere in India, a young married woman is burned alive, beaten to death, or driven to commit suicide".[6] Honour killings are particularly prevalent in parts of Uttar Pradesh, Punjab, and Haryana. Often men and women are killed for transgressing caste barriers – most commonly if a man marries a woman from a higher caste which is often seen as damaging the honour of her caste as a whole. In some cases the motivation for these killings is complicated. For example, in 2004 in the Bhawanipur

1 In 2002, the Human Rights Commission of Pakistan said 376 honour killings were recorded that year in Sindh province. Between January 2001 and December 2004, police recorded 2,228 honour killings in the province. In Pakistan's Punjab province over 1,700 honour killings took place in the five years between 1997-2003, a report by the National Commission on the Status of Women funded by the UNDP said in August 2007. http://www.pakistan-facts.com/article.php?story=20051 127005459809 and http://news.webindia123.com/news/Articles/Asia/20070812/739781.html

2 Oxfam briefing paper, 'Towards Ending Violence Against Women in South Asia' (page 3), August 2004. http://www.oxfam.org.uk/resources/issues/gender/downloads/bp66_evaw.pdf

3 Shirkat Gah, a women's resource centre published in 2001 'The Dark Side of Honour : Women victims in Pakistan' (page 9), by Rabia Ali. http://www.shirkatgah.org/the%20dark%20side%20of%20honour%20-%20bulletin%202001.pdf

4 Amnesty International, 'They Say I Am Kari- So Who Will Protect Me Now?'. http://asiapacific.amnesty.org/apro/aproweb.nsf/pages/svaw_kari

5 Center for Women's and Gender Research, University of Bergen, 'Policing in Purdah: Women and Women Police Station, Peshawar, NWFP, Pakistan', by Farhat Taj. May 2004. http://www.ub.uib.no/elpub/NORAD/2004/uib/thesis01.pdf

6 *Oxfam briefing paper:* 'Towards Ending Violence Against Women in South Asia' (page 3), August 2004. http://www.oxfam.org.uk/resources/issues/gender/downloads/bp66_evaw.pdf

district in Uttar Pradesh, a low caste woman was gang-raped and then killed because her son was said to have run away with the wife of a man from the higher Yadav caste.[7]

Bangladesh: Honour killing is a major problem in Bangladesh. Although even basic statistics are lacking, many believe that several hundred women are killed for honour-related reasons annually.[8] Killings in rural areas are often covered up by families of both the victims and the murderers, the wider community and the local authorities. Police rarely investigate the deaths of women, particularly if their deaths are disguised as accidents and suicides. Furthermore there is also a high genuine suicide rate among Bangladeshi women – largely as a result of verbal, emotional and physical abuse from husbands, brothers, in-laws and other women. As a result, there are now only 100 women to every 105 men in Bangladesh – even though hundreds of thousands of Bengali men have travelled abroad in search of work.[9] This demographic in-balance has reportedly been accentuated by female infanticide, abortion of female foetuses and the widespread practice of giving young girls less food than boys and inferior medical treatment.

7 The Communist Party of India, 'AIDWA Convention Against 'Honour Killings". January 18 2004. http://pd.cpim. org/2004/0118/01182004_aidwa%20convn.htm and *Frontline*, India's national magazine, Volume 21 – Issue 03, February 13 2004. http://www.hinduonnet.com/fline/fl2103/stories/20040213001205000.htm

8 The scale of honour killings can be gleaned from other statistics. Between January and December 2006 there were 639 reported rapes in Bangladesh. Of these, 126 women were subsequently killed and 13 others committed suicide. During the same period there were 243 dowry-related killings reported to the police, Odhikar, a local human rights organization said. http://www.state.gov/g/drl/rls/hrrpt/2006/78869.htm

9 Division for the Advancement of Women: 'Violence against women: A statistical overview, challenges and gaps in data collection and methodology and approaches for overcoming them' (page 2), by Sharmeen A. April 2005. http://www. un.org/womenwatch/daw/egm/vaw-stat-2005/docs/expert-papers/Farouk.pdf

Indeed, in some small, highly-segregated towns in the North and the Midlands, South Asian women may be less likely to suffer honour killings precisely because they are less exposed to non-traditional lifestyles and are therefore likely tempted to transgress their community's cultural boundaries.

Profiling South Asian honour killings

■ *Killings by close relatives and in-laws*

Most victims of honour killings reported in the UK are Muslim women from South Asia who are below the age of thirty. As in other forms of honour-based violence, the majority of killings are carried out either by close family members or husbands.

A typical victim of such honour killings was Samaira Nazir, a 25-year old woman of Pakistani origin. Nazir, a businesswoman and

C A S E   S T U D Y

SIKH WOMAN AT RISK OF HONOUR KILLING

Raj was married at the age of twenty-two in 2002. She is Indian from Punjab. Her husband was 35. She does not speak English. She is currently living in a refuge in the Midlands.

After a year [of marriage] I was forced to receive IVF treatment at the hospital. I was given fertility drugs and fertility treatment from a relative [who was a] family doctor. It was forced [on me] by him and his family, but I think the problem was him and not me.

They made comments all the time; from the father-in-law they were of [an] inappropriate sexual nature and [the] comments from the mother where derogatory, constant put downs; I felt worthless. I got this all the time because he was living with his parents.

Although I had fertility treatment in the UK, they were going to send me to India for special treatment, but I know there was nothing wrong with me and getting treatment there could be dangerous to me, or that would probably be dumped or killed so I had to leave.

Knowing that I [was] about to be sent to India, I packed the same clothes that I had from when I arrived, and went to the police. I got good help from the police and now I have been staying in this shelter for over a month.

Now they don't know where I am and I am worried that if they find out then my life could be in danger. I have spoken to my family back in India, and they are pressuring me to go back into the relationship, but I could never do [that]. I feel ashamed because I have brought shame to the family, because they have told my family and others that I have run off with another man.

I feel that my family are suffering more because they are seen by the community as a failure and [they] are helpless because they can't do anything about – and can't escape – it. There is nothing they can do.

The worst experience is the way my husband treated me; there was no verbal communication for three years and I was imprisoned for five years [in total].

I asked the temple for help and they told me to go back to the family and work at the relationship. I do not trust anyone in the community including the temple because I think people would only help me if it was to their advantage … if my in-laws were like that then I have little faith in the temple or the wider community.

I could never go back home, I won't be accepted by anyone and would be forced to marry again, and probably end up in the same sort of relationship.

university graduate whom friends described as "strong-willed",[22] was summoned to the family home in April 2005 after rejecting husbands proposed by her family and having a relationship with an Afghan asylum seeker. When she refused to stop dating him, her brother (Azhar Nazir, a 30 year-old businessman), her father and her 17-year old cousin, stabbed her 17 times and slashed her throat. Samaira's boyfriend later said:

---

22 *Times Online*: 'Sister is stabbed to death for loving the wrong man', by Steve Bird. June 17 2006. http://www.timesonline.co.uk/tol/news/uk/article675686.ece

Waheed Malik, co-ordinator of Awaaz Asian
Women's Group in Accrington, says:

66 In our culture women are not
allowed to talk about domestic
violence [DV]. If she does talk
about it then maybe the little DV
will become a big DV if the family
thinks that she is talking about it to
outsiders 99

"We were as boyfriend and girlfriend for about five or six years. But
we couldn't tell her family because Samaira said her father was a very
strict man who would not allow any female in his family to marry outside of his caste or tribe. We had discussed marriage. Samaira wanted
to tell her family herself. Her father was very upset and said I was only
after their money."[23]

Samaira's brother and cousin were convicted of murder. Her father fled to Pakistan while on bail and is still wanted by police.
Because there is no extradition treaty with Pakistan, he cannot
be extradited.

Honour killings can be carried out for almost any failure to meet
the expectations of one's in-laws or relatives. Raj, a 27-year old
Sikh woman who is staying in a refuge in the West Midlands, fled
her marital home because she feared that her in-laws were planning to kill her for failing to produce a child. She says:

"Although I had fertility treatment in the UK, they were going to send
me to India for special treatment, but I know there was nothing wrong
with me and getting treatment there could be dangerous to me; that I
would probably be dumped or killed."

Usually, honour killings only take place when a woman's perceived failings become known to the wider community. Only
when the family's loss of honour becomes public knowledge,
does the family finally feel compelled to act. Waheed Malik, co-
ordinator of Awaaz Asian Women's Group in Accrington, says:

"In our culture women are not allowed to talk about domestic violence
[DV]. If she does talk about it then maybe the little DV will become a
big DV if the family thinks that she is talking about it to outsiders."

Shaguftah, a 22-year old Mirpuri Pakistani woman, ran away
from her marital home after being tricked into marrying a mentally disabled man through an arranged marriage. Although she
experienced severe domestic violence from her in-laws during
the marriage, she says that she only became at risk of an honour
killing after fleeing to the refuge where she has lived for the last
14 months. She says:

"They managed to get my number and gave me threatening calls.
They said that they will find me and kill me if I don't return, but the
police found out and got me a new phone. I fear for my life if they
know where I am."

23 *Times Online*: 'Sister is stabbed to death for loving the wrong man', by Steve Bird. June
17 2006. http://www.timesonline.co.uk/tol/news/uk/article675686.ece

C A S E   S T U D Y

GIRL FLEEING FROM HONOUR KILLING THREAT

'Saamiya' is 16-years old girl of Pakstani origin who is currently living in a refuge in the Midlands. Brought up in Birmingham, when she was 16 she was taken to Pakistan and forced to marry after her parents discovered that she had a boyfriend. She was rescued from Pakistan by the FCO's Forced Marriage Unit.

I was taken to Pakistan for a forced marriage when I was 16. My parents found out that I had a boyfriend so I was taken to Pakistan. On the 20th July I got there and on the 21st I was told I would get married – that was three months ago.

I was told of the arranged marriage two hours before the ceremony. I told my dad that I didn't want it but I couldn't do anything – there was no argument. During the Islamic ceremony my dad was standing behind me with one hand on shoulder and with his other hand he had a gun which was pointed at my back so that I didn't say 'no'. To everyone else it looked natural – he was just standing there stroking my shoulder – but just before he had told me that he would shoot me if I didn't go through with it.

After the marriage had gone through, the Foreign Office actually came out to the village and asked me if I wanted to go back. My dad was there so I said no and that I was happy here. But they asked my dad to leave the room and then they asked me again and I said yes, that I wanted to go home.

When I arrived at the airport in England, I had two armed coppers on each side of me and the social services were there as well. Someone had contacted Crime-Stoppers Anonymous so I could get back home. They had phoned up and told the police of all my details about where I lived and that I was going to be taken to Pakistan to get married. I knew the Foreign Office Forced Marriage unit existed but I didn't know how to get hold of them. And when I went to Pakistan I just thought that it was a holiday.

I haven't been back [home] since then. My brothers say that they want to take me back to Pakistan so that they can kill me basically. They'll just pay the police there to keep quiet. The police there are totally corrupt and if they see a girl who's run away they'll take them back to their family. Even when the Foreign Office people came, the [Pakistani] copper wanted to stay with me while they talked to me but they even sent him away so that they could talk to me without anyone hearing of it.

I don't want to be killed! I'm only 16. I want to live my life yet. The thing is that if it all gets worked out, and if I go back and marry who they say, then they're not bothered. My brother said to me when I ran away before that if I come back I can marry who I want. But why should I? Why can't I just marry whoever I want?

Many women are discouraged from fleeing abusive situations because they know that if they are subsequently found by their families, they will be at risk of even greater violence.

■ *Women's involvement in murder*

Honour, as it exists in parts of the Middle East and South Asia, is a cultural concept shared by all members of the community. Consequently women, as well as men, have taken part in honour killings in order to defend their family's honour and to preserve their culture against outside influences.

In 2006, Mohammed Riaz killed Caneze Riaz, his wife and their four daughters in Accrington, Lancashire. Riaz was angered that his wife was speaking out for women's rights and encouraging their daughters to wear western fashions. John Paton, manager of the Lancashire Family Mediation Service, who knew Caneze Riaz, says:

66 He was illiterate and didn't speak any English and he became jealous of his wife who was brought up here. She was very well-respected in the community and did a lot of talks and was much liked. And sadly this man couldn't cope with this and he set light to her house, killing her and her children. It's a tragic case and although it's a rather extreme one it's also largely typical of the sort of problems that arise in these cases **99**

In 1999, for example, Rukhsana Naz, a 19-year old woman of Pakistani origin living in Derby, was murdered by her mother. She was killed when, three years after she had been forced to marry an older man, she became pregnant after having an affair with a young man she had known since childhood. When she refused to have an abortion, her mother told her that she was "an insult to [her] husband".[24] Soon afterwards Naz was held down by her mother while her brother strangled her. Olivia Madden, client co-ordinator for Panah refuge in Newcastle, says:

"It is common for a mother to be involved and we have had a case where a woman was responsible for the killing. We have had women come here running away from home thinking that their mother is going to kill them."

In other cases, honour-killings have been arranged by female in-laws. In 1998 Bachan Athwal, a Sikh grandmother arranged for her family to murder Surjit Athwal, her 27-year old daughter-in-law. Athwal urged her relatives to murder Surjit, a customs officer at Heathrow, after discovering that she was having an affair and was planning to divorce her son. She lured Surjit to India under the pretext of a 'family wedding' where she was killed. After the murder, Bachan boasted that her daughter-in-laws' body had been disposed of in a river.[25] To disrupt police investigations, Surjit and her son (the dead woman's husband) sent forged letters to the Indian police.[26] She was only convicted in July 2007, aged 70 and was sentenced to life.[27]

■ *Role of religion and caste*

In many cases of honour killings by people of South Asian origin, the violence was sparked by relationships which transgressed caste or religious boundaries in a way which was seen as shameful for the individual's family.

In November 2002, for example, Mustaq Ahmed, a 40-year old London businessman of South Asian origin, killed his daughter's boyfriend, Rexhap Hasani, an Albanian Catholic asylum seeker, because he did not want her to marry a Christian. He killed Hasani after he had previously tried and failed to force the couple

---

24 *The Observer*: 'Love, Honour and Obey – Or Die' by Jason Burke. 8 October 2000 http://observer.guardian.co.uk/international/story/0,6903,379174,00.html

25 *Daily Mail*: 'Grandmother jailed for life over honour killing of 'cheating' daughter-in-law'. 19th September 2007.http://www.dailymail.co.uk/pages/live/articles/news/news.html?in_article_id=482669&in_page_id=1770

26 *The Guardian*: 'Sikh wife's 'disgrace' sparked killing, court told', by David Ward. 3 May 2007. http://www.guardian.co.uk/crime/article/0,,2071126,00.html

27 *BBC*: 'Life for murder plot grandmother' 19 September 2007 http://news.bbc.co.uk/1/hi/england/london/7002404.stm

to end their relationship – even though Hasani had changed his name to a Muslim one and promised to have an Islamic wedding.[28] Ahmed was a successful entrepreneur who owned a factory in East London. His background and the background of the victim strongly suggest, in addition to the differences over religion, differences in the two men's relative social status were also an important factor in the killing.

Workers in women's refuges say that some of their clients have been threatened with death by their families because they suspected them of having relationships which transgressed traditional caste boundaries. Sana Bukhari, a support worker for Ashiana, a refuge in Sheffield, says:

> "There is a case in Darnall [a suburb of Sheffield] that I am dealing with, where it involved two boys that grew up here and are educated. Just a few weeks ago because their sister wanted to marry out of the caste they seemed to go crazy about it. They have gone to the stage where they bought guns and the person who wanted to marry their sister had to leave town in fear of his life."

In other occasions, religious ideas of 'right and wrong' behaviour seem to have helped justify honour killings. For example, on 28 June 2001 in Manchester, Faqir Mohammed, a 69-year old Pakistan man who had lived in the UK for thirty years, came back from Friday prayers at the local mosque and discovered his daughter Shahida in her bedroom with a boyfriend. After the boyfriend jumped out of the window, Mohammad grabbed his daughter in a headlock and stabbed her 19 times in the stomach with a knife. When Mohammad stood trial for murder, his lawyer told the court that he was a "strict Muslim" who had hoped to see all his daughters have arranged marriages in Pakistan.[29]

Many women in refuges who have fled violence similarly report that religion was used to justify the use of violence against them. 'Ayesha', a Muslim woman of Pakistani origin who fled home after nearly becoming the victim of an honour killing, says:

> "My husband would always say to me that I was going to hell … He would say that I am going to hell because I was not a good wife for him I did not cook enough for him; 'you didn't have sex with me' he'd say."

---

28 *BBC*: 'Life for 'honour killing". 7 October 2003.http://news.bbc.co.uk/1/hi/england/london/3172202.stm

29 *BBC*: 'Father jailed over daughter's murder'. 18 February 2002. http://news.bbc.co.uk/1/hi/england/1827623.stm

■ *Killings by extended families*

In several cases, women have been killed by their extended families without the consent of their more immediate relatives. This may often provoke further violence from relatives who disagree with the legitimacy of the honour killing.

C A S E   S T U D Y

VIOLENCE FROM IN-LAWS

Shaguftah is a 22-year old woman who was born and brought up in the Mirpur region of Pakistani origin. When she was 19 she was forced to marry a man of Pakistani origin who lived in the UK. Less than two weeks after the wedding and coming to the UK, she began to suffer violent abuse from her husband and his relatives.

When I first met him, my husband was living in Pakistan for two or three months; he was praying and behaving in a proper way. Everyone thought, Mashallah, what a good boy. But in the UK he was not religious, he never prayed, he shaved off his beard, and he didn't do anything Islamically.

My husband was related to me, he was my mother's cousin through her aunt. I didn't have a choice; you don't say yes or no, you just do as you are told. Pretty much from birth you grow up to believe in that mentality, to follow it and teach your children the same thing.

I can't remember the amount of times I was abused; it was a daily thing with my husband, his mother and sister getting involved. Sometimes an iron [was] thrown at me, but not by my husband; he only used to punch and kick me.

After a month of being in the country my husband gave me an Islamic divorce and his mother forced me to marry the younger son who was disabled with the mental age of five. He was eighteen and could not talk or communicate or do anything around the house.

At first I refused, and the beating got worse and worse. They would say things like 'how dare you', and claim that I was being ungrateful and didn't appreciate the great life they were giving me.

The wedding to the disabled child was arranged three times, but something always came up that delayed it, like him going to hospital because of his disability or me being bed ridden through abuse.

In the end, I just left. One day one of the children left the bathroom tap on all night and there was a mess in the morning. I cleaned it up, but when my mother-in-law found out she started hitting me and then pushed me down the stairs. I was semiconscious, but that didn't stop her hitting me around the head with her shoes 'till I completely passed out.

They would never take me to the doctor ever, even after the severest of beatings. Honour stopped me from going back or telling my parents. So I decided to run away.

I was scared at first; they managed to get my number and gave me threatening calls. They said that they will find me and kill me if I don't return, but the police found out and got me a new phone. I fear for my life if they know where I am.

In moments in anger I feel let down by everyone, my parents my culture his parents, but in reality my parents wanted the best for me.

In January 2003 21-year old Sahjda Bibi was killed by her Pakistani cousin, Rafaqat Hussain, on her wedding day. Hussain killed her because he was angry that she had earlier refused to marry his own cousin and because he thought that the wider family was dishonoured by her choice of husband, a divorced father with a child from his previous marriage. Bibi's immediate family had initially opposed the marriage but later accepted her decision and played no part in the honour killing. This murder indicates how pressure on women to conform comes not only from immediate family but also from extended relatives. Similarly, the staggered nature of immigration into the UK means that however much some individuals want to integrate, they can be held back by more recently arrived members of their community who see them as 'selling out' to 'western' culture – as well as by people in their country of origin. Jas, a Sikh woman graduate from Birmingham, says:

> "My aunt got a divorce four years ago after eight years of abuse by her husband. Her family thinks she has brought shame and has dishonoured them. Since then she has faced numerous death threats from the family. When she went to India she had to avoid Punjab altogether because she would definitely have been killed there. Now she is in love with a Muslim guy, so the problem could get worse."

In some cases, disputes over the validity of an honour killing can spark further violence in Asian communities – illustrating that the idea that women should be killed in order to preserve a group's honour is far from universal. For example, in 1999 Haq Nawaz Khan from Walsall, shot dead his half-brother 'Big Ali' Nawaz Khan. The two men had been close until Big Ali had himself shot dead Haq's sister, Shanaz Begum, in Pakistan five months earlier in an honour killing.[30] This uncertainty over what 'justifies' an honour killing means that women are often unable to accurately assess the level of threat they face from angry relatives; often they are inclined to fear the worst. The manager of a woman's refuge and outreach programme in Bradford, who wishes to remain anonymous for safety reasons, says:

> "Every girl that comes here fears that her life could be in danger for whatever reason. They feel like they are fleeing for their lives."

In some cases, women have been killed after going home – unaware that their family had already decided to kill them.

---

30 *Birmingham Evening Mail*: 'Man given life for murder of brother', by Amanda Geary and Louise Grifferty. 1 February 2001.

C A S E   S T U D Y

A MAN WHO WAS KIDNAPPED BY HIS RELATIVES

Imran Rehman is a 33-year old of Pakistani origin who was kidnapped and imprisoned by his relatives in an attempt to force him into a marriage. He was brought up in Birmingham and is now a support worker at the Karma Nirvana refuge in Derby.

When I was ten I was taken to what I thought was a party but it was actually my engagement. There were a lot of people dressed up in traditional Pakistani clothes and people were giving me lots of gifts. In fact I was getting engaged to my uncle's daughter. I was ten at the time; she was five. At the age of fifteen I was shown the photos and was told it was my engagement party and that this five-year old girl was going to be my wife. I was just gob-smacked. I couldn't believe it. I said to my sister, 'you've got to be joking, right?', but she said, 'you've got no choice'. I was told I had to get married. I freaked out and just said I'm not going to do it. I thought that as long as I was in the UK nothing could happen to me.

By seventeen I had been expelled from two schools. Also I got involved in drugs and crime and had a lot of problems. I guess I went off the rails as a way of rebelling. At age seventeen I was asked by my mother if I wanted to go to Pakistan. My sister said 'come to see where your dad was born'. It all sounded ok so I went. The first three weeks were great; the best holiday ever. Three weeks later I was in my Nan's house in Gujarat. I was woken up at five o'clock in the morning by my brother-in-law. He gave me two small tablets and some water. He said to take them and so I did; I thought nothing of it. He said that they would wake me up so that we could go for prayers at the mosque around the corner. I went outside and there was a car there with two men in it – one of them was an imam. I got in and they locked the doors. At that point there were tears running down my face but I fell asleep.

I was woken up with water splashed on my face. Several men were around me; two men held my arms and others held my legs. My brother-in-law said it was time to rehabilitate me. I was mostly swearing at them; threatening them in English. But they shackled my one leg to the other with a metal bar in between and a big ball at the back so that I couldn't walk. Every day I had to wear these metal shackles; I had to eat in the shackles, bathe in the shackles. Every time I went to the toilet eight of them followed me to make sure that I didn't try to escape. There were only three or four houses; no road. Every night I put a chair against the door so that I didn't get sexually abused – but that never happened, luckily. There was a nine-year old kid who was there who I was able to make friends with. He came to me and asked 'why are you shackled up, who have you killed?' I had told him that I hadn't killed anyone. After a few days this kid got me a metal bar which I could use to break the lock on my shackles.

I waited until the moment was right and then I escaped. Because I had been staying in Pakistan I had a friend there in a town called Sialkot. I went there and his dad took me to a doctor who bandaged my foot which had been cut when I escaped. My family would have known that I had escaped from the mosque. Eventually I phoned them up and so I ended up meeting them at the airport. My sister was there with her family; my friend was there with his family – he was from a powerful family and there were lots of them so it was ok. I got my passport and my ticket back and got on the plane. On the whole journey I didn't say one word to my sister. Since then we've talked and she said that she did it to make me a better person. Police were knocking on my door every other week and so my mum said 'send him to Pakistan'. Mum could see all the trouble that I was causing and that I needed rehabilitating. She knew that this was a way to cure me or me otherwise I'd get locked up.

■ *Pre-planned attacks*

Most honour-killings committed by South Asians are planned in advance by one or more members of the victims' family. The pre-meditated nature of such attacks helps distinguish such murders from more spontaneous 'crimes of passion' which are common in many other communities.

In March 1998, Rukhsana Naz, a 19 year-old woman of Pakistani origin, was killed by her mother and 22-year old brother after she threatened to divorce the man she had been forced to marry and said she was pregnant by another man.[31] Three weeks before the murder, Naz's mother confronted her daughter, kicked her in the stomach and ordered her to have an abortion. When Naz refused, the mother made plans with her sons to kill her. The week before her murder, Naz's family forced her to sign a will giving them guardianship of her two children in the event of her death. Naz was strangled by her brother while her mother held her legs.[32]

Many honour killings have a ritualistic element. In April 2005, Samaira Nazir, a 25-year old Muslim woman, was killed in her family's home in Southall, London, by her brother, Azhar Nazir, and her cousin after she refused to marry any of the men proposed by her family. When her family told her she would have to marry a man of their choice, she replied that she wanted to marry her Afghan boyfriend and threatened to leave home, saying to her mother, "You are not my mother anymore". Her brother and cousin then held her down, stabbed her 17 times and cut her throat. They then forced her two sisters – aged two and four – to watch her die. As her brother was led away by police he told them:

> "There had been a problem with my sister. She does not wish to have an arranged marriage. We only allow marriage within the family. My sister wanted to run away from the house and was stopped."[33]

Nazir was a graduate from Thames Valley University and was working as a recruitment consultant. She may have felt that she had outgrown her family's traditions. Her success may also have created feelings of envy among her less successful male relatives; and to have made them feel emasculated by her success and in-

Ghazala Razzaq, the centre co-ordinator at Roshni Asian Women's Resource Centre in Sheffield, says:

66 Some young children as old as 14 will tell their mothers what is acceptable when their fathers are not around because they are taught to act in that way **99**

---

31 *BBC*: Man confessed to murdering sister 11 May 1999 http://news.bbc.co.uk/1/hi/uk/341238.stm

32 *The Independent*: 'Mother murdered pregnant daughter' by Kate Watson-Smyth. 26 May 26 1999

33 *BBC*: 'Man convicted of murdering sister'. 16 June 2006. http://news.bbc.co.uk/1/hi/england/london/5087702.stm

dependence. It is probable that her nieces were forced to watch her murder so they would know not to embrace a 'western' lifestyle as she had. The fact that her killing was carried out by her younger male cousin is also significant. In many cases, South Asian boys are taught by their families from an early age that their duty is to police their female relatives. Ghazala Razzaq, the centre co-ordinator at Roshni Asian Women's Resource Centre in Sheffield, says:

> "Some young children as old as 14 will tell their mothers what is acceptable when their fathers are not around because they are taught to act in that way."

The ritualised nature of Nazir's murder recalls other cases. When the Kurdish teenager Heshu Yones was killed, her father stabbed her eleven times in the chest and then cut her throat,[34] a powerful gesture which for many rural immigrants has connotations of sheep being slaughtered. The manner of killing may reflect deeply internalised views of women as an asset or form of property.

■ *Killing of children*

In some cases, a husband's attack on his wife has resulted in the death of their children. In some cases this is done intentionally if male relatives believe the children have been tainted by their mother's supposed immorality.

In 2006 in Accrington, Lancashire, Mohammed Riaz, an immigrant from Pakistan's highly conservative North-West Frontier Province, killed Caneze Riaz and her four daughters by setting fire to the family home after locking them inside. The girls who died in the blaze were aged 16, 15, 10 and three. The husband, who died from injuries sustained in the fire, had arrived in the UK aged 32 after his wife was sent from the UK to Pakistan to get married. At the time of the killing, the father was under great pressure as his only son, a 17-year old, was in hospital undergoing treatment for leukaemia. Although he had previously criticised his wife for encouraging their children to wear 'western' fashions, the final straw came when his eldest daughter told him that she wanted to become a fashion designer. It seems likely that Riaz felt emasculated both by his failure to produce a healthy son but also by his wife's success; while he worked in a succession of low-paid jobs, his wife was confident and successful, building her own circle of friends and starting to work with women who

---

34 *BBC*: 'Honour killing' father begins sentence'. 30 September 2003. http://news.bbc. co.uk/1/hi/england/london/3149030.stm

```
C   A   S   E       S   T   U   D   Y
```

WITNESS TO AN HONOUR KILLING

Shazia Qayum's best friend was killed at the age of 12 in 1992. Qayum is now a team leader at the Karma Nirvana refuge in Derby.

Me and my friend Saminna used to have a half-day at school every week in the timetable. But we didn't tell our parents so that we could do what we wanted during this time. One day we had this day off which we spend in the park. One of Saminna's family walked through the park and saw us sitting there on a bench. He went back and told her dad that he should go and get her because she had been talking to some boys in the park who were playing football. When her father walked through the park towards us he had one hand threateningly in his jacket like he had a weapon. He came to us and started dragging her away by the hair. After that I panicked and went to the school to tell the teachers what had happened.

In order to get home I had to walk up the street. But the street was sealed off by the police. I didn't know what had happened. I thought that she was in big trouble and would get a good beating for not going to school. It turned out that he had killed her. Her mother and Yasmina [her sister] were at home when he came home with Saminna. He said that she had brought dishonour on the family and that there was no way to restore the honour. He shot at the wife who tried to get in the way, then he shot Yasmin and Saminna. Yasmin died later in hospital. And then he killed himself. And that was when I was 12. We had planned to go to college together; to go to uni together; we did everything together. People would use what happened to Saminna as a threat. They said 'you know what will happen if you don't go to school.'

It's sort of bizarre that she was killed like this; I was forced into a marriage and now all my work is focused on this issue. It's sort of like she's looking down on me.

felt oppressed by traditional South Asian values.[35] John Paton, manager of the Lancashire Family Mediation Service, who knew Canaze Riaz, says:

"He was illiterate and didn't speak any English and he became jealous of his wife who was brought up here. She was very well-respected in the community and did a lot of talks and was much liked. And sadly this man couldn't cope with this and he set light to her house, killing her and her children. It's a tragic case and although it's a rather extreme one it's also largely typical of sort of the problems that arise in these cases."

In July 2006, Uzma Rahan, 32, and her three daughters were killed in Manchester by her husband after he suspected her of having an affair. She came to the UK through an arranged marriage in 1992 but gradually adopted an increasingly 'western' lifestyle, making friends independently and dressing less conservatively. This behaviour gradually enraged her husband, Ra-

---

35 *Telegraph*: 'Father Kills Family for Being too Western', by Nigel Bunyan. 22 February 2007. http://www.telegraph.co.uk/news/main.jhtml?xml=/news/2007/02/21/nmuslim21.xml

han Arshad, who worked as a taxi driver. Under this pressure the couple separated and then reunited. Soon afterwards, Uzma's husband accused her of having an affair and then killed her by hitting her 23 times with a rounders bat before similarly attacking his children.[36] Before her death, Uzma had told her friends that she feared becoming the victim of an honour killing, saying, "Count the days before he kills me."[37] At his trial, Arshad told the court that he had been angered by his wife's decision to wear tight jeans and tops. He said:

> "It wasn't right for a mother and someone who came from Pakistan to change the way she dressed all of a sudden. It wasn't right at all."[38]

'Saamiya', a 16-old girl of Pakistani origin from the Midlands, says:

66 My brothers say that they want to take me back to Pakistan so that they can kill me basically. They'll just pay the police there to keep quiet. The police there are totally corrupt and if they see a girl whose run away they'll take them back to their family ... 99

Sometimes children are killed accidentally in honour-related attacks. In Aston, Birmingham, in March 2006, a six-year old girl, Alisha Begum, was killed after her family's house was fire-bombed by the Bengali relatives and friends of a 16-year girl who her brother was dating. Mohammed Foaz Ahmed, the girl's brother, and his friend Jabed Ali are still wanted by police for the attack and are believed to have fled to Bangladesh.[39] Two of their friends, Hussain Ahmed, a 26-year old dentist, and Daryll Tuzzio, 18, were convicted for their part in the attack.

■ Killings abroad

Frequently, women are killed after being taken 'home' to the Indian subcontinent. Often their families appear to hope that the police there will not investigate the case properly. These killings further show that many honour killings are pre-meditated and planned in advance.

In 1998 Bachan Athwal, a Sikh woman was taken to India and killed by her in-laws because they believe that she was planning to get a divorce. They were only convicted in 2007 after one of the victim's relatives gave fresh evidence to the police. Police said that securing a prosecution had been complicated because Athwal's body was never found – it had been reportedly dumped

---

36 *Manchester Evening News*: 'Uzma Arshad: The Westernised wife'. 13 March 2003. http://www.manchestereveningnews.co.uk/news/s/1001/1001816_uzma_arshad_the_westernised_wife.html

37 *Stockport Express*: 'Evil dad slaughtered wife and three kids', by Barbara Simpson. 14 March 2007http://www.stockportexpress.co.uk/news/s/524/524561_evil_dad_slaughtered_wife_and_three_kids.html

38 *Stockport Express*: 'Arshad: Profile of a killer'. 14 March 2007. http://www.stockportexpress.co.uk/news/s/524/524550_arshad_profile_of_a_killer.html?related_link

39 *Birmingham Mail*: 'Firebomb murder suspects 'may be back'', by Mark Cowen. 31 October 2007.http://icbirmingham.icnetwork.co.uk/mail/news/tm_headline=Hunt%20for%20firebomb%20murder%20suspects&method=full&objectid=20038646&siteid=50002-name_page.html

in an Indian river.[40] In other cases, women are believed to have been taken abroad to be killed simply because their husbands have become bored of them and want to re-marry without having the shame of getting a divorce. A worker in a woman's group in northern England, who asked to remain anonymous, says:

> "It does not matter to them; they are just objects that can be thrown away, no matter who they are. They get rid of women by sending back to Pakistan. We have had one here, who was sent back, and subsequently killed by her family for trying to re-marry as that brought shame to the in-laws' family."

"Saamiya", a 16-old girl of Pakistani origin from the Midlands, who requested anonymity due to safety concerns, says:

> "My brothers say that they want to take me back to Pakistan so that they can kill me basically. They'll just pay the police there to keep quiet. The police there are totally corrupt and if they see a girl whose run away they'll take them back to their families... I haven't been back [to my family]. I don't want to be killed! I'm only 16. I want to live my life yet."

There are no reliable figures on how many British women have been taken abroad and killed.

Kurdish honour killings

The Kurdish regions of Iraq and Turkey have among the highest rates of honour killing per capita recorded. According to some estimates, as many as a thousand women in Iraqi Kurdistan are killed by their families every year.[41] In Turkey, Kurds, who make up no more than a quarter of the population, carry out a disproportionate number of honour killings.[42] A 1999 survey of women in predominantly Kurdish south-eastern Turkey found that 74 per cent of rural women believed that their husband would kill them if they had an affair.[43]

---

40 *BBC*: 'Murder without a body of evidence', by Debabani Majumdar. 19 September 2007. http://news.bbc.co.uk/1/hi/england/london/7002853.stm

41 The UN has reported that during the first half of 2006 alone, more than 500 women were killed in Iraq's Kurdish regions alone. Similarly, in June 2007, a police chief reported that "one or two" honour-killings were reported every day in Erbil province http://www.dailystar.com.lb/article.asp?edition_id=10&categ_id=2&article_id=22666 (page 10). http://www.uniraq.org/FileLib/misc/SG_Report_S_2006_360_EN.pdf and (page 15) http://www.uniraq.org/FileLib/misc/HR%20Report%20Apr%20Jun%202007%20EN.pdf

42 *AFP*: 'Honour killings, feuds claim nearly 1,200 lives in Turkey'. 4 March 2006.

43 *Pinar Ilkkaracan and Women for Women's Human Rights*: 'Exploring the Context of Women's Sexuality in Eastern Turkey' (page 72). http://www.wluml.org/english/pubs/pdf/dossier22/women-sexuality-turkey.pdf

Nazir Afzal, from the Crown Prosecution Service, says:

66 These cases resonate beyond the immediate family as we often deal with cases where significant members took part in the act; in the murder. And in the case of Banaz [Mahmod], for instance, in addition substantial numbers of the community actually did not assist and support prosecutors; instead they supported the family members who were responsible for the killing. They really didn't care and it showed … We don't see this as domestic violence – it's beyond that. The murder of Banaz was so brutal that it was a clear warning to others; it was a way of saying 'don't step out of line or this could be you' 99

Despite the frequency of honour killings by Kurds in parts of Iraq and Turkey, there are relatively few recorded cases of honour killings by Kurds in the UK. Only two Kurdish women are recorded as having been killed by their relatives in the UK (Heshu Yones and Banaz Mahmod). However because at least two other Kurdish women living in the UK (Shawbo Ali Rauf and Subhia Nadir) have been taken back to Iraqi Kurdistan and killed there, many Kurdish women's organisations believe that the number of Kurdish women living in the UK who have been killed could be higher. The relatively low numbers of known Kurdish honour killings may also conceal how widely honour killings are seen as acceptable by Kurdish immigrants in the UK. For example, some Kurdish women's groups in London estimate that 10 per cent of the women who flee to refuges believe themselves at risk of being killed.[44]

■ Kurdish women killed for becoming 'western'

In all four known cases of Kurdish women living in the UK being killed, all were murdered on suspicion of having boyfriends – which their family members and the community iterpreted as a sign of becoming 'westernised'. In all cases, the women's deaths followed years of physical and emotional violence committed either by close family members or by the men they had been forced to marry.

Abdulla Yones killed his daughter, Heshu, in October 2002 after subjecting her to months of repeated beatings in an unsuccessful attempt to force her to end her relationship with her boyfriend, an 18-year old Lebanese Christian. He finally killed her after her relationship became public knowledge among the Kurdish community of North London and he received a note at his work at the offices of the Patriotic Union of Kurdistan saying that his daughter was a prostitute.[45] Soon afterwards he found a stash of love letters in his daughter's room and a note that showed she was planning to run away. Later recovered by the police, one letter read:

Bye Dad, sorry I was so much trouble.
Me and you will probably never understand each other, but I'm sorry I wasn't what you wanted, but there's some things you can't change.
Hey, for an older man you have a good strong punch and kick.

---

44 For example, Diana Nammi, director of Iranian and Kurdish Women's Rights Organisation in London, believes that one in ten women who come to her refuge believe themselves to be at a risk of an honour killing.

45 *The Daily Telegraph*: ;Muslim cut his daughter's throat for taking a Christian boyfriend'. By Sue Clough and Sean O'Neill. 30 September 2003 http://www.telegraph.co.uk/news/main.jhtml;sessionid=0EL53AIWUAVSPQFIQMGSM5OAVCBQWJVC?xml=/news/2003/09/30/nyones30.xml

I hope you enjoyed testing your strength on me, it was fun being on the receiving end.
Well done[46]

After killing his daughter, Abdulla unsuccessfully tried to kill himself by slitting his own throat and then jumping off his balcony. It is unclear whether he attempted suicide from remorse or to avoid punishment. Six months before her killing, her father had taken her to Iraqi Kurdistan where he had put a gun to her head and demanded if she had a boyfriend. He had then forced her to undergo a gynaecological examination to prove that she was a virgin.[47]

In 2006 another Kurdish woman, Banaz Mahmod, was killed after leaving the Kurdish husband who she had been forced to marry, aged 16, and falling in love with an Iranian man from a different Kurdish clan. Her father had attempted to kill her on a previous attempt but had not succeeded. Banaz's numerous attempts to alert the police failed and a policewoman, PC Angela Cornes, dismissed her account as "dramatic and calculating". Banaz's family had previously attempted to kill her older sister, Bekhal, for acting like a 'westerner' by smoking and using hairspray. After her sister's murder, Bekhal described her father's attempts to force her to abandon her 'western habits':

"One day I was walking home through the park and I'd taken my scarf off and my father saw me. He screamed at me: 'Who do you think you are? You are acting like a bitch.' He pulled me inside the house, spat in my face and then picked up his slippers to beat me around the head as he shouted: 'Don't you ever disobey me.' In the two years before I ran away, I think he beat me more than 20 times. It would be over silly things like undoing the top button of my school shirt, or using hair gel. Once, he picked up a metal soup ladle and hit me round the head repeatedly with it. I didn't want to have boyfriends or go out at night or anything like that. I was respectful to my parents. I just wanted to be able to have friends, to give my opinion, very small things that British girls take for granted."[48]

In all the known cases involving Kurds in the UK, the women were killed by their older male relatives or men paid to come from abroad to carry out the murder.

46 *BBC*: 'Honour killing' father begins sentence'. 30 September 2003. http://news.bbc.co.uk/1/hi/england/london/3149030.stm

47 *Chicago Tribune*: 'For family honor, she had to die'. December 18 2007. http://www.chicagotribune.com/news/specials/chi-0511170188nov17,0,5040345.story?page=3

48 *Daily Mail*: 'Honour killing' sister breaks her silence', by Helen Weathers. 17 June 2007. http://www.dailymail.co.uk/pages/live/femail/article.html?in_article_id=462342&in_page_id=1879

C A S E   S T U D Y

LETTER FROM AN HONOUR KILLING VICTIM

In 2003, Heshu Yones, a 16-year old Kurdish girl in London wrote wrote several letters in which she said that she was planning to run away from home. When her father discovered the letters, he killed her. One letter reads:

"Goodbye Mum, I will see you again one day. Thank you a thousand times for trying so hard for me. I'm sorry I was such a bad friend. Some day I will try and make it up to you. Keep letting off that gas in your fat stomach. Enjoy life—now that I'm gone, there's no more trouble. I promise you I will be good.

Bye Dad, sorry I was so much trouble. Me and you will probably never understand each other. I'm sorry I wasn't what you wanted, but there's some things you can't change. Hey, for an older man you have a good strong punch and kick. I hope you enjoyed testing your strength on me; it was fun being on the receiving end. WELL DONE.

The time has come for us to part. I'm sorry that I have caused so much pain, but after sixteen years of living with you it is evident that I shouldn't be a part of you. I take all the blame openly—I'm not the child you wanted or expected me to be. DISAPPOINTMENTS ARE BORN OF EXPECTATIONS. Maybe you expected a different me and I expected a different you.

One day when I have a proper job every penny I owe you will be repaid in full. I will find a way to look after myself. I will go to social security to get myself a flat or hostel. I will be okay. Don't look for me, because I don't know where I'm going yet. I just want to be alone. But I will be safe. So have a nice day, have a nice week, have a nice life, because the biggest problem in this house has now left.

Bro, I'm not leaving you forever, just for a little while. I'm sorry to do this to you. I LOVE YOU MORE THAN I KNOW WHAT THE WORD LOVE MEANS. PLEASE FORGIVE ME!!! My problem has always been too much talk, too little action. So goodbye. One day you will see that I will make something good of myself. This isn't an end, it's just a new beginning, so enjoy. I'll come and visit you at school, as often as I can. So you'll be seeing a lot of me, okay?

LIFE, BEING HOW IT IS, ISN'T NECESSARILY HOW IT IS. IT IS JUST SIMPLY HOW YOU CHOOSE TO SEE IT.

GOODBYE & GOOD LUCK."

Source: *Harper's Magazine*: 'Chronicle of a death foretold'. (January 2004). http://www.harpers.org/archive/2004/01/0079871

■ *Killers arriving from Kurdistan/Kurdish women being killed abroad*

Kurdish honour killings often have an international component. Women may either be taken abroad to be killed or else their family might arrange for relatives from Kurdistan to come to the UK to carry out the killing.

In May 2007, 19-year old Shawbo Ali Rauf was taken from her home in Birmingham to Iraqi Kurdistan. Once there, her family stoned her to death after finding unknown numbers on her mobile telephone which they thought proved that she was having an affair. When her husband returned to the UK, police refused to prosecute him – despite demands from Kurdish women's groups. In a similar case, in 1999 Pela Atroshi, a Swedish Kurd, was taken to her family home in Dohuk, Iraqi Kurdistan, where she was shot dead by her uncle on suspicion of having a boyfriend.[49] There could be other cases which have not been recorded. Sawsan Salim, co-ordinator of the Kurdistan Refugee Women's Organisation in North London, says:

> "We don't know how many go back and get killed, we are not sure."

In many Kurdish cases, murders are carried out with the full consent of the victim's extended family. The Mahmod family agreed to kill Banaz during a meeting attended by members of their extended family in their home in South London. After the murder, carried out by two extended family members flown in from Iraqi Kurdistan, Banaz's body was buried in a garden in Birmingham and the local community told police that Banaz was not missing and said that she was from a "liberal" family who would not have killed her.[50] Nazir Afzal, the lead on honour-based violence at the Crown Prosecution Service, says:

> "These cases resonate beyond the immediate family as we often deal with cases where significant members took part in the act; in the murder. And in the case of Banaz, for instance, substantial numbers of the community actually did not assist and support prosecutors; instead they supported the family members who were responsible for the killing. They really didn't care and it showed."

Women's groups also say that young Kurdish men living in the UK can also easily be hired to track down or attack fugitive women on behalf of the family. Sawsan Selim, co-ordinator of the Kurdistan Refugee Women's Organisation, says:

> "There are a lot of disadvantaged people here. If you give one of these men a photo and £2,000 to kill someone they will do it. It is a lot of money for these people if you are only on two or three pounds an hour."

Two of the men wanted for the killing of Banaz Mahmod returned to Kurdistan shortly after the murder. The Kurdish Re-

Sawsan Selim, co-ordinator of the Kurdistan Refugee Women's Organisation in North London, says:

66 There are a lot of disadvantaged people here. If you give one of these men a photo and £2,000 to kill someone they will do it. It is a lot of money for these people if you are only on two or three pounds an hour **99**

---

49 Amnesty International report: Iraq: 'Decades of suffering, Now women deserve better' http://web.amnesty.org/library/pdf/MDE140012005ENGLISH/$File/MDE1400105.pdf and http://web.amnesty.org/library/Index/ENGMDE140012005?open&of=ENG-IRQ

50 *Daily Mail*: 'Murder girl's five cries for help that were ignored', by Fiona Barton'. 12 June 2007. http://www.dailymail.co.uk/pages/live/articles/news/news.html?in_article_id=461280&in_page_id=1770&in_a_source

gional Government has said that it knows the men's identity but the British government has said that it is unable to extradite the men due to the lack of a relevant extradition treaty.[51]

■ *Ritualised nature of Kurdish honour killings*

In many cases, Kurdish honour killings have a strong ritual element. Often the murder itself and the events leading up to it seem intended to degrade the victim and to present the murder as an act of collective justice.

When the 19-year old Shawbo Ali Rauf was taken from her home in Birmingham to Iraqi Kurdistan and killed in May 2007, her relatives stoned her to death. This 'Islamic' execution was presumably intended to portray the murder – both to the woman and other family members – as a legitimate act that was both culturally and religiously permissible.

Similarly, Banaz Mahmod was punished before her death with rape and beatings designed to deliberately humiliate her. On the orders of her father, she was stripped by her killers and raped for two hours in her family home before being garrotted. Mohamad Hama, a 30-year old Kurd recruited by Banaz's father to kill her, was recorded telling a friend in prison that he had "slapped" and "fucked" the 20-year old woman as her father watched.[52] The ritualised nature of such abuse makes it clear that such killings are seen by elements in the Kurdish community as quasi-judicial punishments with a strong moral dimension rather than as spontaneous outbursts of anger. Often, such ritualised brutality suggests these killings are intended as a warning to other women not to transgress the community's moral 'red lines'. Nazir Afzal, the lead on honour-based violence at the Crown Prosecution Service, says:

> "We don't see this as domestic violence – it's beyond that. The murder of Banaz was so brutal that it was a clear warning to others; it was a way of saying 'don't step out of line or this could be you'."[53]

Two of the Kurds who carried out honour killings in the UK have

---

51 *The Guardian*: "Honour' killing: pressure grows on UK to extradite suspect from Iraq', by Karen McVeigh. 22 November 2007. http://www.guardian.co.uk/Iraq/Story/0,,2215030,00.html

52 *Chicago Tribune*: 'For family honor, she had to die', special report. 20 December 2007. http://www.chicagotribune.com/news/specials/chi-0511170188nov17,1,358759,full.story

53 This motive was openly articulated by Muslim and Middle Eastern writers as early as 1860 when Mela Mehmud Bayezidi, a Kurdish scholar, wrote in an essay called 'Kurdish Manners and Customs' that the purpose of honour killings was to instill fear in other women to make them guard their modesty and their chastity. http://www.womansrights.org/doc/FadimeMojab.pdf (page 3)

often fought in conflicts in Iraqi Kurdistan. Such experiences may have left them psychologically damaged by encouraging them to view extreme violence as commonplace and socially acceptable. For example, Ari Mahmod, who arranged for relatives to kill his daughter Banaz Mahmod, was an ex-soldier in the Iraqi army.[54] Abdulla Yones, who killed his daughter Heshu in Acton, had taken part in the Kurdish uprisings of the 1980s and early 1990s.

Arabs and others

Honour killings are common in all parts of the Arab world. However the data is often incomplete as few Arab governments allow surveys of gender-based violence.[55] Despite this, substantial evidence suggests that the practice is widespread. Some reports estimate that as many as 300 honour-killings may occur annually in Syria,[56] 30-40 in Jordan, around 10-12 annually in the Palestinian territories[57] as well as dozens in other countries such as Yemen and Iraq. Honour killings by Arab Christians have also occurred in Egypt[58] and the Palestinian territories.

Despite this widespread violence towards women, there have been no recorded honour killings by Arabs in the UK – even though many women's groups say that domestic violence among Arab immigrants is common. Mona Elogeali, outreach worker at Al Husaniya, one of the few refuges dealing specifically with Arab women says:

> "I have not come across honour related killings. I have come across forced marriages, but it is mainly arranged marriages, love marriages and couples who have run away."

Some say that Arabs in the UK do not carry out honour killings because they can force women to comply with cultural and re-

Numerous women's groups say that the rates of forced marriage and domestic violence among Arab communities in the UK are lower than in South Asian ones. Mohamed Baleela, a team leader at the Domestic Violence Intervention Project in Hammersmith in West London, says:

66 I think that the Arabic-speaking community deal with it in a different way ... They remove their families back home and then they think 'problem solved'. Once the women are back, they will have to do what they have been taught. Even if they are not forced to marry a particular person, they will still marry someone from their own community 99

---

54 *The Times*: 'Having fled Iraq, she died at the hands of her father' by Steve Bird. 12 June 2007. http://www.timesonline.co.uk/tol/news/uk/crime/article1918019.ece

55 Attempts to survey violence against women in the Arab world – and in the wider Middle East – disproportionately cover relatively open countries like Egypt, Jordan and Yemen. The problem may be equally acute in countries like Saudi Arabia, Syria and Libya where comparable data is currently not available.

56 *The New York Times*: 'A Dishonorable Affair', by Katherine Zoepf. September 23 2007. [http://www.nytimes.com/2007/09/23/magazine/23wwln-syria-t.html?pagewanted=1&_r=1&adxnnlx=1197896704-zsV9V%20zicZUq/Bi0hjl9ow

57 Amnesty International: 'Israel: Conflict, occupation and patriarchy: Women carry the burden'. http://web.amnesty.org/library/pdf/MDE150162005ENGLISH/$File/MDE1501605.pdf and The Jerusalem Post, 'Report: Palestinian 'honor killings' up', by Khaled Abu Toameh. 29 May 2007. http://www.jpost.com/servlet/Satellite?cid=1180450951435&pagename=JPost%2FJPArticle%2FPrinter

58 UN office on drugs and crime – Division for Advancement of Women: 'Violence against women: Good practices in combating and eliminating violence against women'. 20 May 2005. http://www.un.org/womenwatch/daw/egm/vaw-gp-2005/docs/experts/khafagy.honorcrimes.pdf

C A S E   S T U D Y

A male honour killing victim: Arash Ghorbani-Zarin

In November 2004, Arash Ghorbani-Zarin, a 19-year old of Iranian descent studying at Oxford Brookes University, was killed by the Bangladeshi family of his girlfriend, Manna Begum, after she refused to break off her relationship with him.

The girl's father Chomir Ali, 44, told his British-born sons Mohammed Mujibar Rahman, 19, and Mamnoor Rahman, 16, to kill Ghorbani-Zarin after finding out that the girl was pregnant and that the couple had intended to marry. The girl's family were particularly provoked by the couple holding hands and kissing in public. Speaking at the trial of Chomar Ali and his sons, Manna Begum's close friend, Cheherazad Jmil, said:

"She [Manna] would walk around the streets holding hands [with Arash]. I warned her not to do it because it would bring shame on her family ... Muslim girls should not date. I told her not to embarrass her family by doing so ... It's just the way Muslims are; the girls do not date. It's shameful for the family."

Shortly before her boyfriend was killed by her family, Manna Begum attempted to slit her wrists because she could not cope with the pressure from her family who allowed her brothers to enjoy a western lifestyle. Mujibar, the girl's older brother who played the lead role in her murder, drank alcohol, had girlfriends and regularly went clubbing, for example. After the murder of her boyfriend, the girl's family forced her to travel to Spain to get a late-term abortion. Both of the boys who were convicted for the murder were brought up in the UK.

Source: *The Times*: 'This Muslim girl defied her father – and her lover paid with his life', by Daniel McGrory. 5 November 2005. http://www.timesonline.co.uk/article/0,,2-1858245,00.htm

ligious codes through other means. Mohamed Baleela, a team leader at the Domestic Violence Intervention Project in Hammersmith in West London, says:

"I think that the Arabic-speaking community deal with it in a different way ... They remove their families back home and then they think 'problem solved'. Once the women are back, they will have to do what they have been taught. Even if they are not forced to marry a particular person, they will still marry someone from their own community."

A similar situation prevails in the UK's Turkish community. Although up to 200 men and women die in honour-based violence occur every year in Turkey, no honour killings have been recorded among Turks living in the UK. Derya Yildirim, a Turkish project co-ordinator for Refuge's community outreach project in London, says:

"Turkish communities in North London have tried to resolve issues themselves by interfering and not by going to the police. There was a recent case where a Turkish woman who was married had an affair with a black man and she had a mixed race child. Her husband found out only in the hospital. When they heard about this the community group interfered to protect her and they gave her money to leave the country. But this is a temporary measure – this is not a structured approach and it is not really a solution."

There are also no known incidences of honour killings by Soma-

C A S E   S T U D Y

DUMPED IN PAKISTAN

'Khan' was married at the age of 17 to her cousin. She comes from Karachi, Pakistan. She was married to a British-born graduate and businessman of Pakistani origin who lived in Slough.

My husband was British, and had his British home with his family. So I moved to England in 1998 to 2003. I have three children. First one the girl, born in Saudi Arabia, then my daughter and son who is the youngest also born in the UK. I don't do papers for residency because I didn't know and I spoke little English.

I was a house wife, looking after my children and looking after my husband's family in Slough. I was mistreated very badly. Not just my husband but his whole family was very bad, and they were my relatives. Didn't have anyone, I spoke no English.

All the time they just treated me as a slave; I cooked, cleaned and looked after the kids. I was treated as a slave, beaten by my husband and women in the family would pull my hair. They would do things if dinner is late – the whole family – and this happens a lot with Asian families.

When my husband re-married [married a second wife], he married here. He just had Nikah. My children didn't get treated well, he would push them [sometimes]. When my husband' new lady came, she would sleep with him while I slept down stairs. He did not ask me if he wants to marry.

He refused to divorce and would use to hit me. I was not allowed to speak to my mom or any of my relatives in Pakistan. I wasn't allowed to speak to anyone, leave the house or have friends.

Then suddenly he said 'Oh... you have not spoken to your mother in so many years, don't you want to see her? I have tickets'.

In the summer of 2003 we went to Pakistan, just he and me. I was very happy to see my mother, sister and brothers [Father is deceased]. He said we go Pakistan just for two weeks. I tell him why you do not bring children with us. He made so many excuses. I never suspected he would leave.

He dropped me at my mother's house in Karachi. One week later he phoned me and tells me he is in the UK now. I say what about me, he said after one month I come and take you. I say where is my passport, and he said, 'Tickets in Pakistan are very expensive'. I asked about my children and he told me not worry. My daughter said, 'when you come back?' and I said, 'tell your daddy to come and take me'.

One month became two then three, he kept delaying and delaying. For one and a half year I was in Pakistan with no money and without my three children. There was no honour or shame in my family. My mother was all the time praying for me, she was supportive and all my two brothers and sisters.

Finally he said that he will come and pick me and bring the children, so I packed my suitcase a month before just waiting. But he did not come. So in January 2005 I went to the High Commission office in Karachi. It took 5 months to arrange my return, from January to May.

lis in the UK. In Somalia, honour killings are rare – even though ideas of sexual honour are strong and women are often seen as less valuable than men.[59] Fathiya Yusuf, Somali community outreach worker for Refuge's office in Deptford in South East London, says:

Fathiya Yusuf, Somali community outreach worker for Refuge's office in Deptford in South East London, says:

66 From hearing stories, honour killing does not exist in Somalia but there is dishonour instead. A woman who gets pregnant without getting married or who runs away or becomes a prostitute; she becomes an outcast 99

"From hearing stories, honour killing does not exist in Somalia but there is dishonour instead. A woman who gets pregnant without getting married or who runs away or becomes a prostitute; she becomes an outcast. For the family it is as if she is dead but they won't go as far as killing someone. It's not allowed – it's considered illegal as far as religion is concerned. But if the family won't talk to her and they dishonour her, she will be made to feel ashamed by the whole community. Unless she leaves the community altogether or goes to another country she will have a hard time for her whole life."

Men as victims of honour killings

Although the victims of honour-killings are usually women, around 10-20 per cent of South Asians killed in honour-based violence in the UK are men.[60] Typically men are killed for having a relationship with a South Asian woman by her relatives who wish to avenge the damage done to their family's honour.

As in cases involving women, men are usually killed only once news of the affair becomes public knowledge and the woman's family feel they have exhausted all other options. Often the killing seems to be an act of public revenge and, thanks to at least partial endorsement by the community, can send out a strong warning message to men from other communities.

Honour killings of men are not triggered exclusively by pre-marital and extra-marital relationships, but can be carried out in response to almost any violation of sexual or social codes. On 23 September 2005, for example, Mohammed Shaheen, the co-owner of a taxi firm in Chorlton, Manchester, was shot-dead by Khyber Khan, his brother-in-law. Khan, 28, had flown to Manchester from Pakistan to kill Shaheen after his sisters had told him that he had sexually assaulted them. After the killing, Khan's sisters helped him flee the country – he was eventually arrested in Canada and deported to the UK.[61]

59 For example, according to a 2002 report by UNICEF, in many parts of Somalia the blood money due for killing a man is 100 camels while a woman's is 50 camels. (Page 15) http://www.unicef.org/somalia/SOM_WomenInIslam.pdf

60 Based on a CSC analysis of 40 honour-related crimes committed between1990 and 2007.

61 *The Asian News*: 'Gun killer's revenge over sex attack allegations'. 26 January 2007. http://www.theasiannews.co.uk/news/s/522/522818_gun_killers_revenge_over_sex_attack_allegations_.html

In some cases, violence between members of different religious groups can be caused by women and honour. In August 2004, a gang of Muslim men mistakenly attacked Major Singh Gill, a 45-year old Sikh man, because they believed – wrongly – that his son was dating a Muslim. The six Muslim men burst into Gill's shop in West Bromwich in the West Midlands and beat him to death with iron bars, clubs and hockey sticks.[62] Two of the killers later fled to Pakistan.

There are few, if any, cases of honour killings of white men or women by South Asian families. This might suggest that honour killings are usually carried out against people who are expected to understand Asian social, cultural and religious standards. One of the few exceptions occurred in 2003 when Kalvinder Dosanjh, a Sikh, tried to arrange for a hitman to kill Temple Jazac, a 43-year old Jewish builder, who was having a relationship with Sanjit, his 23-year old daughter. He also tried to arrange for Jazac's father to be killed but failed when he was approached by an undercover policeman while attempting to arrange the hit-job.[63]

It is notable that there are no known cases in the UK of men being killed by their own families for sexual impropriety – underscoring how South Asian cultures see women as upholders of collective values. Men's sexual behaviour – as long as it is heterosexual – is seen as having little bearing on the collective honour of the family group. Imran Rehman, a support worker at Karma Nirvana in Derby whose parents attempted to force him into a marriage, was told that once he was married, the family's pride was satisfied and that his subsequent behaviour was less important:

> "My mother told me that once you're married you can do whatever you want. It's the girl who carries the honour; the pride."

The only possible exception might be in cases of homosexuality. Men suspected of homosexuality are frequently harassed and killed by members of their family and community in South Asia and the Middle East. There are, however, no known cases in the UK of homosexuals from these areas being killed for honour related reasons.

---

62 *BBC*: 'Two guilty over religion killing'. 20 June 2005. http://news.bbc.co.uk/1/hi/england/west_midlands/4637461.stm

63 The rareness of such cross-cultural honour killings indicates the continuity of much honour-based violence throughout the centuries, in particular the understanding that the idea of honour only functions between two people existing in the same conceptual universe. For this same reason, European duels were only fought between men of similar rank and while medieval jousts – in which men competed to win renown for themselves and honour for their ladies – were only fought between knights (Honour and Shame; Pitt-Rivers, page 7).

CHAPTER 5

Female Genital Mutilation

Introduction

Female Genital Mutilation (FGM), also referred to as female circumcision, refers to the partial or complete removal or modification of the female genitalia for cultural or religious reasons. Just as other forms of honour-based violence aim to prevent women from damaging a family or community's honour through their sexual activity, in most cases, female genital mutilation FGM can be seen as an attempt to prevent female infidelity and sexual independence by reducing a woman's sex drive.

Maureen Salmon, the interim-director of Forward UK, a London-based group which campaigns against FGM worldwide says that FGM, like many other forms of honour-based violence, aims to control female sexuality and keep women as virgins until their marriage:

> "There is an honour issue in the sense that one of the reasons for FGM is to guarantee that women will find husbands who see them as eligible for marriage. FGM is carried out to safeguard virginity until marriage. There are cultures which think that if a woman has not been circumcised she is not eligible."

FGM is usually carried out by women (and in particular by the child's grandmother). Often the operation is done without the knowledge of male members of the family. The World Health Organisation (WHO) has estimated that every year around 2 million female children in Africa undergo some form of FGM.[64] It also estimates that around 130 million women worldwide have already undergone the procedure.[65]

The World Health Organisation has defined the main types of FGM as follows:[66]

---

64 Unicef Fact sheet No: 241: Female Genital Mutilation (June 2000) http://www.who.int/mediacentre/factsheets/fs241/en/

65 Unicef: Child Protection Information Sheet: Female Genital Mutilation/Cutting (May 2006) http://www.unicef.org/protection/files/FGM.pdf

66 Unicef Fact sheet No: 241: Female Genital Mutilation (June 2000) http://www.who.int/mediacentre/factsheets/fs241/en/

❖ **Type I** – excision of the prepuce, with or without excision of part or all of the clitoris

❖ **Type II** – excision of the clitoris with partial or total excision of the labia minora

❖ **Type III** – excision of part or all of the external genitalia and stitching/narrowing of the vaginal opening (infibulation)

❖ **Type IV** – pricking, piercing or incising of the clitoris and/or labia; stretching of the clitoris and/or labia; cauterisation by burning of the clitoris and surrounding tissue

Origins of the practice

FGM is based on the idea that a family's honour is rooted in the behaviour, and particularly the sexual fidelity, of its female members. However unlike other forms of honour-based violence which are generally the result of anger and passion, FGM is a closely choreographed ritual that aims to situate a girl within the traditions of her community and its ancestors. Some forms of the practice is believed to date back to Ancient Egyptian times, around 2400 B.C.E,[67] although similar customs have developed independently by different cultures around the world. The practice was also mentioned by Herodotus who said that Phoenicians, Hittities and Ethiopians, as well as Egyptians carried out the practice. The Romans too carried out a version of FGM, passing metal rings through the labia of female slaves to prevent them from having sex.[68] In all cases the purpose of FGM has been carried out in an attempt to control and reduce a woman's sexual desire and to demonstrate patriarchal control over their bodies.

Despite its patriarchal roots and obvious role in controlling females, in many cultures and societies FGM has become such an entrenched part of a culture that many women enthusiastically endorse the practice. The reasons given for this vary; in some case it is believed that uncircumcised women will give birth to deformed children or that uncircumcised women will grow up less beautiful or intelligent; in parts of Sudan it is believed that unless cut off, a woman's clitoris will continue growing until it

Maureen Salmon, the interim-director of Forward, says:

66 There's a lot of anecdotal evidence. For example, I've had a call from a woman in Birmingham who said that her husband wanted to take her six-year old daughter out of the country to Gambia 99

---

67 Source: Internet Ancient History Sourcebook. http://www.fordham.edu/HALSALL/ANCIENT/asbook04.html

68 Female Genital Mutilation edited by Comfort Momoh (page 7) http://www.radcliffe-oxford.com/books/bookdetail.aspx?ISBN=1857756932 and http://www.radcliffe-oxford.com/books/samplechapter/6932/Momoh_01-34fef2c0rdz.pdf

Fathiya Yusuf, the Somali Community
Outreach Worker for Refuge in Deptford:

❝ Growing awareness within the
community is making change and so
is the government saying it is illegal.
It is the combination of these that
is effective. The government making
it illegal stops people doing it; work
within the community tells people
that they don't have to do it **❞**

resembles a goose's neck.[69] In many instances circumcision is seen
as such a normal and inevitable act that the thought of a woman
not being circumcised can produce strong feelings of revulsion
amongst both men and women. In almost all cases a circumcised woman is seen as morally and physically cleaner than one
who has not undergone the procedure. In communities where
FGM is commonplace women who are not circumcised are often
not able to marry. This obliges families to continue circumcising
their daughters for fear they might otherwise end up unmarried
and destitute. In some cultures FGM is so entrenched that some
'western' researchers working in the FGM-prevalent areas of Africa have themselves internalised the practice after being initially
opposed to it. Hanny Lightfoot-Klein, for instance, who has carried out some of the most extensive studies of FGM in Sudan,
argues that the practice is not unduly harmful in medical, sexual
or psychological terms.[70]

Muslim attitudes to FGM

Although FGM predates Islam by thousands of years, for centuries it has been regarded by many Muslims across the Middle East
as an essential religious practice perhaps because one of its main
aims has been to control the sexuality of women – which has also
been a theme of much Islamic scholarship.

Although FGM is not mentioned in the Quran, many prominent
Islamic scholars have endorsed the practice. For instance, the influential 14th century manual of Shaafi law, The Reliance of the
Traveller by Ahmad ibn Naqib al-Misri says that the practice is
"obligatory".[71] The Hanafi and Maliki schools traditionally also
regarded FGM as 'noble'.[72] In most cases these scholars based
their reasoning on hadiths they believed showed Muhammad
approved of the practice.

---

69 Hanny Lightfoot-Klein. "Prisoners of Ritual: Some Contemporary Developments in the
History of Female Genital Mutilation," presented at the Second International Symposium
on circumcision in San Francisco, April 30-May 3, 1991. http://www.fgmnetwork.org/
Lightfoot-klein/prisonersofritual.htm

70 For example see Hanny Lightfoot-Klein *The Sexual Experience and Marital Adjustment
of Genitally Circumcised and Infibulated Females in The Sudan* in The Journal of Sex Research
Vol.26. No.3, pp.375-392 August, 1989. http://www.fgmnetwork.org/authors/Lightfoot-
klein/sexualexperience.htm

71 The Reliance of the Traveller ('Umdat as-Salik wa 'Uddat an-Nasik) trans. by Nuh Ha
Mim Keller (1997) has become increasingly influential among Western Muslims after being
translated by Nuh Ha Mim Keller in 1991. It was the first book of Islamic legal jurispru-
dence in an English language to be certified by al-Azhar university. Although Keller did not
translate some sections dealing with slavery as he considered them irrelevant, he retained
the section advocating female circumcision.

72 Anne Sofie Roald *Women in Islam: The Western Experience*, Routledge, London, 2001 (page
24)

YUSUF AL-QARADAWI ON FGM

On 1 July 2007, Yusuf al-Qaradawi, the spiritual leader of the Muslim Brotherhood, writing on islamonline.net, the English-language website which he oversees, responded to a woman in Egypt who wrote to ask 'What is the Islamic legal ruling concerning female circumcision?' He replied:

"Actually, this is a controversial issue among jurists and even among doctors. It has sparked off fierce debate in Egypt whereby scholars and doctors are split into proponents and opponents.

"However, the most moderate opinion and the most likely one to be correct is in favor of practicing circumcision in the moderate Islamic way indicated in some of the Prophet's hadiths – even though such hadiths are not confirmed to be authentic. It is reported that the Prophet (peace and blessings be upon him) said to a midwife: "Reduce the size of the clitoris but do not exceed the limit, for that is better for her health and is preferred by husbands".

"The hadith indicates that circumcision is better for a woman's health and it enhances her conjugal relation with her husband. It's noteworthy that the Prophet's saying "do not exceed the limit" means do not totally remove the clitoris."

He added that while the practice was not obligatory for Muslims, he believed that it was a justified way to control female behavior "under the current circumstances in the modern world" – presumably a reference to the 'western' ways of life on offer to Muslim women:

"Actually, Muslim countries differ over the issue of female circumcision; some countries sanction it whereas others do not. Anyhow, it is not obligatory, whoever finds it serving the interest of his daughters should do it, and I personally support this under the current circumstances in the modern world. But whoever chooses not to do it is not considered to have committed a sin for it is mainly meant to dignify women as held by scholars."

Source: *Islamic Ruling on Female Circumcision* by Yusuf al-Qaradawi (1 July 2007) http://www.islamonline.net/servlet/Satellite?pagename=IslamOnline-English-Ask_Scholar/FatwaE/FatwaE&cid=1119503543886

In a modern context, attempts to reduce FGM rates have generally been supported by secularist and moderate Muslims and opposed by the more conservative Islamic clerics – although this is not always the case. For instance, in October 1994 Muhammad Sayyid Tantawi, the grand mufti of Egypt, challenged the idea that there were any valid hadiths which permitted FGM or made it compulsory. He was opposed however by opposition Islamists who equated any attempt to challenge traditional customs as an effort to promote 'western' culture and ideas at the expense of Islam. One such challenger was Abu al-Ashbal az-Zuhairi, a Salafist, who published a booklet defending the practice in 1996. He argued that removal of all or part of the clitoris was justified by its goal: "What is intended by female circumcision is to set right her sexual desire, for if she is uncircumcised she would be seized by a strong sexual desire".73 Other anti-government Egyptian clerics such as Sheikh Yusuf al-Badri have also opposed the ban on FGM. In January 2007 Al-Badri said that not circumcising women would cause them to become promiscuous and to bring dishonour on their families. "Circumcising helps the woman control her sex drive. It helps her control herself," he said.74 The practice has also been defended by many of the most senior members of the Muslim Brotherhood [See FACTBOX: *Yusuf al-Qaradawi on FGM*].

But despite the support of many Islamists for some form of FGM, almost all Muslim clerics oppose infibulations (Type III FGM) which they usually regard as an unlawful pre-Islamic practice. In Sudan, for example, where some form of FGM is almost universally practiced in some of the country's predominantly Muslim regions, the practice has been opposed by many leading Islamists. For example, during the Islamist government of Omar al-Bashir, who took power in Sudan in 1989, infibulation was made illegal – although milder form of FGM remained tolerated.[75]

Attitude of other religions

Although most women who are at risk of FGM worldwide are probably Muslim, FGM is also found in non-Muslim cultures and societies – primarily in Africa.[76] In Egypt, the practice is as common among Coptic Christians as among Muslims.[77] Similarly the practice is found in Christian areas of East Africa such as Ethiopia and Eritrea as well as in parts of West Africa where animalist

---

73 Roald, Anne Sofie, *Women in Iskam, Female Genital Mutilation*, Routledge (page 245), London 2001.

74 *McClatchy Newspapers*: Female genital mutilation persists in Egypt despite renewed opposition by By Miret el Naggar and Hannah Allam 25 January 2007 http://www.mcclatchydc.com/staff/hannah_allam/story/15599.html

75 Sudan Human Rights Organisation: *The Situation of Human Rights June 1st – September 30th*, 2003 (Published by the Sudan Human Rights Organisation's Cairo branch http://www.shro-cairo.org/reports/october03.htm

76 For instance, a 2005 report by Unicef noted that in Niger, Nigeria and Tanzania, non-Muslim groups are more likely to practice FGM than Muslim ones. Unicef: *Female Genital Mutilation/Cutting: A Statistical Exploration* (page 10)(Unicef, New York, 2005) p.10 http://www.unicef.org/publications/files/FGM-C_final_10_October.pdf

77 For example, see *Egypt: Demographic and Health Survey*, 2005, by Fatma El-Zanaty and Ann Way March 2006 http://www.measuredhs.com/pubs/pdf/FR176/16Chapter16%2Epd. (page 211-219)

Estimated FGM prevalence rates in England and Wales:

Number of girls under 15 who were estimated to have undergone or be at risk: 98,376

Number of women in UK who have undergone some form of FGM: 65,000

Maternities per year to women who have undergone FGM: 30,487

Number of girls under 15 who have undergone, or are at risk of, infibulations (Type III circumcision):   16,000

Source: *A statistical study to estimate the prevalence of Female Genital Mutilation in England and Wales.* Forward, London, 2007. http://www.forwarduk.org.uk/download/96

---

beliefs are still prevalent. In Egypt, Coptic Christian leaders have stated that the practice has no basis in Christianity and should be stopped. For example, Bishop Moussa, Bishop for Youth of the Coptic Orthodox Church and representative of Pope Shenouda III, the head of the Coptic church, has said:

> "From the Christian perspective – this practice has no religious grounds whatsoever. Further, it is medically, morally and practically groundless. [...] When God created the human being, he Made everything in him/her good: each organ has its function and role. So, why do we allow the disfiguring of God's good creation? There is not a single verse in the Bible or the Old or New Testaments, nor is there anything in Judaism or Christianity – not one single verse speaks of female circumcision."[78]

However, such official disapproval has had a limited effect. Small-scale localised campaigns by Christian priests in rural Egypt have often been more effective. For example, a campaign by the Coptic Evangelical Organisation for Social Services in villages in Upper Egypt produced a "sharp decline" in FGM prevalence in just five years.[79]

Similar strategies have been applied in Ethiopia by groups such as Care Ethiopia and Save the Children Norway-Ethiopia.[80] These efforts have helped reduce prevalence rates. One survey found that in 2000 80 per cent of women had undergone FGM; in 2005

---

78 Unicef: Changing A Harmful Social Convention: Female Genital Mutilation/Cutting (Unicef, Florence, 2007) http://www.unicef-icdc.org/publications/pdf/fgm-gb-2005.pdf p.12

79 Unicef: *Coordinated Strategy To Abandon Female Genital Mutilation/Cutting In One Generation: A Human Rights-Based Approach To Programming* (Unicef, New York, 2007) p.29-30. http://www.childinfo.org/areas/fgmc/docs/Coordinated_Strategy_to_Abandon_FGMC%20_in_One_Generation_eng.pdf]. Also Who Health Organisationl: *Female Genital Mutilation: Programmes to Date: What Works and What Doesn't* (Department of Women's Health, Health Systems and Community Health, World Health Organization, 1999) p.59 http://www.who.int/reproductive-health/publications/fgm/fgm_programmes_review.pdf.

80 *The Norwegian International Effort Against Female Genital Mutilation* by Tonje Bentzen and Aud Talle(Oslo, July 2007) (page15-16) http://www.norad.no/items/8252/38/3520709369/The%20Norwegian%20International%20Effort%20Against%20Female%20Genital%20Mutilation.pdf

that figure had fallen to 74.3 per cent. FGM is most common in Muslim areas in the south and east of the country. In Eritrea, Christians frequently believe that the practice is endorsed in the Old Testament.[81] Some local Christian priests have tried to halt the practice – but often with limited effects.

FGM in the UK

Perhaps even more than other honour-related crimes, FGM is an underground practice and may not even be openly discussed within communities and families. In many cultures men are not aware of the nature of the FGM operations and the suffering that they can cause to women at the time of the operation and in later life. In addition, the very nature of the act means that even in places such as East Africa where the practice is near-universal it is usually carried out in semi-secrecy in private homes. The difficulty of tracking FGM in the UK can be gauged by the fact that since the Female Genital Mutilation Act became law in 2003, not a single person has been prosecuted for the offence. A previous law, the Prohibition of Female Circumcision Act 1985, also failed to produce any prosecutions.

Prevalence

An October 2007 study carried out by Forward and the London School of Hygene and Tropical Medicine estimated that at least 98,376 women under the age of 15 were at risk of undergoing some form of FGM or had already undergone the procedure.[82] Of this, the study estimated that nearly 16,000 girls aged 8 and below were at risk of suffering a Type III mutilation – the most extreme. The study also estimated that around 65,000 women in the UK had already had some form of FGM – most of whom will have suffered it before leaving their home country. Alison Mac-Farlane, one of the co-authors of the report, says however that "we think this is an underestimate" and that the real figures may be higher. Despite this, the figures in the survey are the most accurate to date. The Department of Health had previously estimated that 74,000 women in the UK have undergone the procedure.[83] In both cases, these estimates are based on little more

---

81 *A Study on Female Genital Mutilation In Eritrea* by Worku Zerai. April 2003. http://www. stopfgm.net/dox/worku_zerai_fgm_eritrea_2003.pdf (page 44)

82 *A Statistical Study to Estimate the Prevalence of Female Genital Mutilation in England and Wales (Summary Report)* by Efua Dorkenoo, Linda Morison and Alison Macfarlane (Foward UK, 2007, London) (page 25) http://www.forwarduk.org.uk/download/96

83 See briefing paper *Prevention of Female Genital Mutilation in the UK* issued by the British Medical Association (BMA) in July 2006 http://www.bma.org.uk/ap.nsf/Content/PreventionFGM

than extrapolations based on the number of immigrants from countries where FGM is commonplace. The uncertainty over the numbers of women at risk is shared by those working directly in the field who admit that they have little idea of the scope of the problem. Yet despite the lack of hard-data, women's groups say that there is evidence that it is being practiced on women in the UK on a substantial scale. Maureen Salmon, the interim-director of Forward, says:

> "There's a lot of anecdotal evidence. For example, I've had a call from a woman in Birmingham who said that her husband wanted to take her six-year old daughter out of the country to Gambia. There's a precaution we have at Forward to alert the social services in a case like this. We also have teenagers who were cut five years ago which means that it can only have happened when they were in this country."

She adds that the scale of the problem can only ever be estimated because girls cannot usually report that they have been circumcised for several years or more after the actual event:

> "It's only when they seek medical advice in their teens that we know about it – and it became clear to us that this was done when they were seven. And there's the trouble of getting the information – when they go to the family planning clinic that is confidential for example ... The reason for all these problems is that it's a hidden crime. A child really isn't going to testify against their parents – because it's so personal it will take a lot for a child to even tell their teachers that it happened to them during the school holidays for instance. It's not until they get to their teens and early 20s that the consequences become real to them and they want to speak about it."

In different communities

■ African

Attention on FGM in the UK has mostly focused on immigrants from East African nations where FGM rates run to over 90 per cent. In many parts of Somalia, Sudan and Djibouti rates of FGM are believed to exceed 90 per cent. In some Muslim countries where it is common such as Mali (where 90 per cent of women have undergone FGM) the practice is legal while others (such as Libya and Djibouti) have recently outlawed it. However, in other mainly Muslim countries in Africa such as Niger less than 5 per cent of women have undergone FGM. In some occasions followers of non-Muslim African religions such as animists in Benin and Orthodox Christians in Ethiopia also practice FGM. Despite this, anecdotal evidence suggests that, among African immigrants

Jenny Moody, the chairperson of Luton Women's Aid, a refuge, says:

66 We get girls who have been threatened with FGM, and that's why they left. The most recent one was a Muslim Zimbabwean, and aged 18. She escaped. We had 3 cases so far 99

and their descendents in the UK, support for carrying out FGM on their children – especially in its more extreme forms – is declining rapidly.

For example, while surveys in Eritrea suggest that around 80 per cent of women aged 15-18 have been mutilated, Eritrean women's workers in the UK say support for the practice is declining rapidly among Eritreans in the UK.[84] Saba Melles, an advice worker at the Eritrean Community Centre in Islington in London, says:

> "Because of over 30 years of war, many Eritreans have been displaced for so many years so they didn't have much chance to practice their own culture and that has also helped the people in exile give up these traditions. Now I don't think we have such an issue with FGM because of so long a period of being in exile, people have come out of it. I don't say 100 per cent have stopped the practice in the UK but it's much less common than in Eritrea where it is still accepted."

Even in the Somali community, sometimes noted for its insularity, attitudes are changing rapidly – even though FGM remains common in Somalia.[85] Fathiya Yusuf, the Somali Community Outreach Worker for Refuge in Deptford, says:

> "We are starting to realise that it's just culture; it's not religion; Islamically we're not allowed to do it ... Growing awareness within the community is making change and so is the government saying it is illegal. It is the combination of these that is effective. The government making it illegal stops people doing it; work within the community tells people that they don't have to do it."

Despite this overall change, however, there are scattered reports of operations being performed overtly in the UK or on children taken 'back home'. Yusuf says:

> "In this country I haven't come across people doing it but I have heard horror stories of children being taken back to have it done there. It's preferable to have it done when children are very young; if you try and do it later maybe the woman will try to fight people off to stop them doing it. When children are around seven years old their parents may take them back to Somalia and they have it done there – but I've never come across it being done here."

---

84 *A Statistical Study to Estimate the Prevalence of Female Genital Mutilation in England and Wales (Summary Report)* by Efua Dorkenoo, Linda Morison and Alison Macfarlane (Foward UK, 2007, London) (page 17) http://www.forwarduk.org.uk/download/96

85 *A Statistical Study to Estimate the Prevalence of Female Genital Mutilation in England and Wales (Summary Report)* by Efua Dorkenoo, Linda Morison and Alison Macfarlane (Foward UK, 2007, London) (page 17) http://www.forwarduk.org.uk/download/96

Jenny Moody, the chairperson of Luton Women's Aid, a refuge, says that she has also seen some cases of women threatened with FGM – but says that these may just be the tip of the iceberg:

"We get girls who have been threatened with FGM, and that's why they left. The most recent one was a Muslim Zimbabwean, and aged 18. She escaped. We had 3 cases so far. I think it's there but for some reason we are not picking it up."

■ *Arab*

Information about FGM in the Arab world is scarce – however this does not mean that it does not happen. Just as in the case of honour killings and other sensitive issues, independent surveys on FGM in the Arab world have only been carried out in the few countries which are sufficiently open. Where such surveys have been carried out they have revealed that FGM is much more common than was originally anticipated. In Egypt, for example, surveys found that that over 90 per cent of women (both Muslim and Christian) have undergone some form of FGM[86]. Efua Dorkenoo, a Ghanian campaigner against FGM who co-founded Forward, says:

"It's only African countries where governments have really opened this up to study. Other countries, particularly Arab ones, have not and so we don't know what's going on there."[87]

In Yemen, one of the few other Arab countries where FGM prevalence has been studied, surveys suggest that at least a quarter of women have undergone some form of FGM.[88] However, in many cases, the form of circumcision differs and may escape detection. For instance, in the Yemen's coastal Tihama region where links with Africa are strong, up to 70 percent of women may have undergone FGM – often in the Africa style.[89] There are also scattered reports of FGM occurring in the United Arab Emirates

---

86 *A Statistical Study to Estimate the Prevalence of Female Genital Mutilation in England and Wales (Summary Report)* by Efua Dorkenoo, Linda Morison and Alison Macfarlane (Foward UK, 2007, London) (page 17) http://www.forwarduk.org.uk/download/96

87 Speaking at the launch of Forward's FGM Prevalence Study in England and Wales on 9 October 2007.

88 Unicef Yemen FGM/C Country profile. Briefing paper published by Unicef in November 2005 http://www.childinfo.org/areas/fgmc/profiles/Yemen/Yemen%20FGC%20profile%20English.pdf

89 ibid.

(UAE), Libya and Saudi Arabia.[90] In the 1990s, for example, a survey carried out in the UAE suggested that 30.8 per cent of girls between the ages of 1 and 5 had been circumcised.[91] Government hospitals there have been prohibited from performing the procedure since 1996, but the practice likely continues to occur. There are also reports that 'western' women married to local men in the UAE have been threatened with FGM in attempts to ensure their sexual subservience to men and their compliance with local customs.[92] Surveys of Bedouin Arabs in southern Israel have also found that FGM – mainly Type I – is common among certain tribes where all girls are required to undergo the procedure, usually when aged between 12 and 15, in order to be considered eligible for marriage. Researchers have noted however that "no exact numbers are available, as the Bedouin are reluctant to relinquish information on the ritual and resent inquiries into intimate aspects of their culture".[93]

■ *Kurdish*

Apart from Egypt and Yemen, one of the few areas of the Arab world where FGM incidence has been surveyed is Iraq's Kurdistan region. Although FGM was known to be practiced there, the practice was believed to be rare. However in 2005, Wadi, a German charity, surveyed 116 villages in the Iraq's Kurdistan region and found that 65 per cent of the 3665 women interviewed had undergone FGM.[94] Researchers from Wadi found that Kurdish villagers who had circumcised their daughters cited religious reasons, for example, saying that if a girl is not mutilated "even the

---

90 *Harvard International Review*: 'No end in sight: female mutilation unabated' by Rebecca Buckwalter. Spring 2005. http://hir.harvard.edu/articles/1310/ *Arab News*: 'Female Circumcision: Weight of Tradition Perpetuates a Dangerous Practice' by Maha Akeel. 20 March 2005 http://www.arabnews.com/?page=9&section=0&article=60703&d=20&m=3&y=2005&pix=community.jpg&category=Features

91 Freedom House Country Report: United Arab Emirates (page 185) http://www.freedomhouse.org/template.cfm

92 Agence France Press: Abused women find shelter in controversial UAE refuge by Ali Khalil 17 May 2006. Avaiable at http://www.metimes.com/International/2006/05/17/abused_women_find_refuge_in_controversial_uae_shelter/7737/

93 U Elchalal, B Ben-Ami, A Brzezinski Female circumcision: the peril remains BJU International, Volume 83, Issue S1, (1999), 103–108. http://www.blackwell-synergy.com/action/showPdf?submitPDF=Full+Text+PDF+%2876+KB%29&doi=10.1046%2Fj.1464-410x.1999.0830s1103.x&cookieSet=1 It is perhaps worth noting that, as regards Israel's Bedouin, FGM occurs alongside with some of the world's highest recorded rates of domestic violence. For example, one 2003 study of 202 Bedouin women found that 48 percent had suffered "lifetime exposure to domestic violence" See: 'The Physical and Psychosocial Health of Bedouin Arab Women of the Negev Area of Israel: The Impact of High Fertility and Pervasive Domestic Violence' by Julie Cwikel, Rachel Lev-Wiesel and Alean Al-Krenawi in Violence Against Women, Vol. 9, No. 2, 240-257 (2003) http://vaw.sagepub.com/cgi/content/abstract/9/2/240

94 2 July 2007 press release by Wadi: http://www.wadinet.de/news/dokus/press_june07-stopfgm_en.htm. Also see Middle East Quarterly: Is Female Genital Mutilation an Islamic Problem? by Thomas von der Osten-Sacken and Thomas Uwer Winter 2007 http://www.meforum.org/article/1629

water she carries back from the well will be 'haram'."[95] The high incidence of FGM in Kurdistan closely tallies with that region's exceptionally high rates of violence against women. The large-scale immigration of Iraqi Kurds into the UK since the mid-1990s means that it is likely FGM is being carried out among Kurdish communities in Britain. Kurdish women's groups in the UK say that they have come across evidence of the practice being carried out among Kurds in the UK. Sawsan Salim, co-ordinator of the Kurdistan Refugee Women's Organisation in North London, says:

> "FGM is a major problem. Kurdistan has become the second worst after Africa; 3200 cases so far in some recent research. One volunteer [in London] came to me and told me that a woman has requested three daughters to get circumcisions soon as they get their British passport. With my generation this never happened. This came after 1991. This is happening to Kurdish women going back, but I don't know if it is happening here."

■ South Asian

FGM is rare in Pakistan, Bangladesh and India – although surveys are again incomplete. The only South Asian group known to habitually practice FGM are the 100,000 Bohra Muslims who live in Pakistan and the Gujarat region of India. However the absence of reliable surveys of women's sexual health – especially in Pakistan, Bangladesh and remote regions of India – make it impossible to say whether the practice is more widespread.

Although FGM is rare in South Asia, some women's groups in the UK believe that the practice may now be occurring among South Asians in the UK. Shaminder Ubhi, director of the Ashiana network in Leyton, says that she has come across cases of South Asian girls in their early teens who have reportedly been threatened with circumcision by their families:

> "I have girls threatened with it, but we have probably dealt with one or two in our history."

Although such cases are rare, in this context it seems that FGM may be used by some South Asian immigrants in the UK – like other forms of violence against women – to control the sexuality of their family's women and to enforce traditional standards of female behaviour.

---

95 *IRIN news agency*: Iraq: Survey suggests widespread female circumcision in Kurdish north 6 January 2006. http://www.irinnews.org/report.aspx?reportid=24541

■ *Other groups*

FGM is increasingly believed to be more widespread in parts of Indonesia than was previously realised. In some cases, Indonesian-style FGM is more ritual than real involving only a small symbolic cut but in other cases Type I or II operations are carried out. In 2000 during Muslim attacks on religious minorities in Indonesia's Maluku Islands, thousands of Christian women (and men) were forcibly circumcised by Islamist clerics as part of their forcible conversion to Islam.[96] There is no information on whether the relatively small numbers of Indonesians living in the UK are practicing FGM on their children.

---

96 *Sydney Morning Herald*: 'Terror attacks in the name of Religion', by Lindsay Murdoch, 27 January 2001.

77

CHAPTER 6

Barriers to change

Introduction: the reinforcing of traditional attitudes

Honour-based violence in the UK is no longer simply the result of first-generation immigrants bringing their values with them when they arrived. Instead the idea that the honour of an individual or a family depends on the behaviour of one's women is now being sustained from generation to generation within the UK. It is also now common for third or fourth generation immigrants to play a key role in reinforcing traditional codes of behaviour over other members of their family and community, including in some cases over their parents. Some have even participated in the honour killings of their female siblings.

In general, social and cultural attitudes largely develop through the interaction between an individual and their family, community and peer groups. For example, a woman's understanding of her role in community is programmed at an early age through how her parents treat her – and particularly how they treat her in relation to her male siblings. These attitudes may then be further reinforced through future interactions with extended family members, neighbours and schoolmates – and with community figures such as local elders and religious leaders. Jasvinder Sanghera, director of Karma Nirvana, a refuge in Derby, says:

> "These families are conditioning their girls to believe that it's unacceptable to talk to a guy; to have a boyfriend. And at the same time boys are getting told that it's their duty to keep an eye on their sisters and to make sure that they do not step out of line."

Many factors influence how a person's value system evolves. However, it is broadly clear that families and communities in the UK where honour-based social systems are proving slowest to change are those which have least direct contact with non-traditional behaviour patterns. In other words: where families mix less with other ethnic or religious groups their children have fewer opportunities to experience alternatives to traditional ways of life compared to those who live in a more mixed area, or compared to children who are themselves of mixed parentage. Children brought up in such a mono-cultural environment are consequently less likely to absorb and practice non-traditional values themselves in later life.

Jasvinder Sanghera, the director of the Karma Nirvana refuge in Derby, says:

66 There is this sheer reluctance by people to integrate; people are almost being encouraged not to integrate; the idea of integrating goes against everything that they have ever been taught 99

78

The extent to which the values of children differ from those of their parents are not only affected by the dynamics of the relationship between children and their immediate relatives however. Many immigrant groups – especially those from Muslim parts of South Asia – have taken a number of steps, both consciously and unconsciously, individually and collectively, to prevent their children from abandoning traditional ways of behaviour. These include importing socially-conservative marriage partners from abroad, adopting self-segregating patterns of settlement, choosing conservative religious leaders and councillors who will defend and reinforce traditional attitudes from above and sending children to after-school religious classes. Women who, despite being deliberately sheltered from outside influences, break or threaten to break traditions are also subjected to a number of penalties – including, but not limited to, honour-based violence – which are intended to force them to conform to traditional roles.

Community attempts to block change

Many immigrants have made ideas of honour and female chastity one of the core parts of their individual and collective identities. While honour-based violence is perhaps the most dramatic way in which concepts of female behaviour are enforced, communities have also erected a range of barriers which aim to control and condition women from an early age.

■ Imported wives and husbands

The practice of bringing wives and husbands into the UK from traditional and conservative parts of the world is probably the largest cause of the perpetuation of traditional attitudes and thereby of honour-based violence.

Shahien Taj, director of the Henna Foundation in Cardiff, says:

66 Families bring in both brides and husbands to enforce their social and traditional values on their daughters and sons because they believe it is right **99**

Families and communities give many reasons for importing men and women from abroad for marriage such as the tradition of marrying first cousins or of honouring promises made to family members in the country of origin. However, one of the main reason parents want their children to marry an imported spouse is usually to ensure that they do not become 'westernised' and so their grandchildren will be brought up in a traditional environment. Jasvinder Sanghera, director of the Karma Nirvana refuge in Derby, says:

"There is this sheer reluctance by people to integrate; people are almost being encouraged not to integrate; the idea of integrating goes against everything that they have ever been taught."

79

A primary aim of importing spouses is to slow down and prevent integration and to reinforce and perpetuate traditional attitudes. Kubir Randhawa, director of the Asian Family Counselling Service in Southall, says:

> "They think they are going to lose something [if the woman marries outside the community] and they want to retain their culture, so families think they should marry from within their own relatives. It often happens to girls when they are 15-16 just before they go to college because the family is scared that girls will marry or meet someone not from their community."

In many cases, families know that by importing women for husbands, traditional values will be perpetuated because the wife will play the primary role in instilling values in the future generation. Similarly men can be brought from abroad to impose traditional values on women who are becoming 'westernised'. Shahien Taj, director of the Henna Foundation in Cardiff, says:

> "Families bring in both brides and husbands to enforce their social and traditional values on their daughters and sons because they believe it is right."

Mohamed Baleela, a team leader in the Domestic Violence Intervention Project in Hammersmith, says that many Arab Muslim families also import husbands if they fear that their daughter will marry a non-Muslim and thus potentially have children who are not Muslim, thus perpetuating religious segregation:

> "If a girl falls in love with a guy at college and he is not a Muslim, the family will object to the marriage – definitely. They will probably force her to stop seeing him and marry someone else."

In many communities where marrying people brought in from abroad is common, some observers say that attitudes towards women, honour and domestic violence have scarcely changed in several decades. Despite outward appearances, they say, third- and fourth- generation immigrants hold views that are as traditional – and sometimes more traditional – than those of their parents. Waheed Malik, the co-ordinator of the Awaaz Asian Women's Group in Accrington, says of younger generations:

> "Of course they speak English and their attitude is different to their parents; in general, in their outlook, body-language and general appearance they are different to their parents. But at the same time they still learn their culture because of their community and their parents. When this changes we can see real changes. But this varies from town to town also. In Manchester, people will say the new generation has

Mohamed Baleela, a team leader in the Domestic Violence Intervention Project in Hammersmith, says:

❝ If a girl falls in love with a guy at college and he is not a Muslim, the family will object to the marriage — definitely. They will probably force her to stop seeing him and marry someone else ❞

MIDDLE EASTERN LAWS WHICH DISCRIMINATE AGAINST WOMEN

Almost all Middle Eastern countries have laws which discriminate against women. These laws help to promote a view that men are superior to women. Many immigrants from the Middle East bring such ideas with them when they come to the UK.

Syria: Article 548 of the law code states that if a man witnesses a female relative committing an immoral act and then kills her, he should not be prosecuted.[1]

Lebanon: Law 562 of Lebanon's penal code reduces sentences for men guilty of honour crimes while law 522 pardons any rapist who marries his victim.[2]

Egypt: Article 17 of the Personal Status law allows judges to reduce sentences in cases where a murder may have been provoked. This has resulted in perpetrators of honour killings receiving sentences of as little as six months. Article 277 of the same law states that a man is only guilty of adultery if it is committed in the marital home; a woman is guilty of adultery wherever the act is committed.[3]

Kuwait: Article 153 of the penal codes reduces sentences in cases of honour-killings.[4]

Yemen: Article 40 of the Personal Status Act No. 20, 1992 mandates a wife's obedience to her husband, including by restricting her movements outside the marital home, and by requiring her to have sexual intercourse with him. Article 242 of law No. 12/1994 says that men who find their wife in the act committing adultery and kill her should receive a maximum of year in prison or a fine.[5]

1 *The New York Times*: 'A Dishonorable Affair' by Katherine Zoepf. 23 September 2007. Source: http://www.nytimes.com/2007/09/23/magazine/23wwln-syria-t.html?_r=1&pagewanted=1&oref=slogin

2 *The Daily Star* (Lebanon), 'Coalition raises awareness of outdated laws permitting marriage and rape' by Jessy Chahine (22 July 2005).

3 Khafagy F, 'Honour Killing in Egypt' .Expert paper prepared by Fatma Khafagy, The Association of Legal Aid for Women, for the United Nations Division for the Advancement of Women. http://www.un.org/womenwatch/daw/egm/vaw-gp-2005/docs/experts/khafagy.honorcrimes.pdf

4 Human Rights Watch Kuwait: Promises Betrayed: Denial of Rights of Bidun, Women, and Freedom of Expression. October 2000, Volume 12, Number 2(E). http://www.hrw.org/reports/2000/kuwait/kuwait-05.htm

5 Sisters Arab Forum for Human Rights Honor Crimes in Yemen: A legal & social analysis on violence against Yemeni women pertaining to honor. May 2005, Yemen.

changed a lot – they choose their own marriages, they are educated; they buy their own houses away from their parents. But because Accrington is very small, things have not changed a lot."

Women's groups interviewed say that such stagnation often appears to be more common in smaller, highly segregated northern towns like Accrington, Rotherham and Bradford than in larger cities like Manchester or London where immigrants and their descendents are exposed to a wider range of ideas and lifestyles.

■ Segregation and self-segregation

The development of mono-cultural and mono-ethnic ghettos in parts of many British cities plays a key role in perpetuating traditional attitudes and slowing down the spread of 'western' ideas such as sexual equality.

Just as many communities tacitly endorse honour-based violence, so many of the same communities also see the growth of mono-cultural ghettos as a positive development which will allow them to better preserve their values and traditions from outside interference and influence. Nazir Afzal, the Crown Prosecution Service's national lead on honour-based violence, says:

> "There are areas in some northern towns you can go to which are road-after-road, street-after-street of villages transplanted directly from South Asia where everyone knows everybody else's business; everyone knows everyone's secrets. Why do people choose to live like that? Because it's convenient, because they like it; because they want to be near their family; because they want to feel like they have some sort of security against the wider community; against the world outside. They haven't really understood what being British is about – and they don't want to. In some northern towns there are real horror stories – from places like Blackburn where people say that you might as well be in rural Kashmir for all the way that women are seen and treated."

Others see the development of such areas as less negative phenomenon. Atif Imtiaz, a community worker in Bradford,[97] says:

> "If you drove through the town in the 80's it would have looked more diverse than it is today. You might think it is segregation, but it is not the case, people grow up and want to live next to their family; that's chain migration. Sons and daughters live close to their parents when they marry or move out because in Asian cultures there is always a link between the families."

Debbie Fawcett, the manager of the Hydburn and Ribble Valley Outreach women's group, which is based in Accrington, says:

❝ On one hand it is a small community and everyone knows everyone. But at the same time once you're accepted by the community leaders and it is clear that they support you, then you're in. The downside of this is that if you upset them you are out **❞**

---

97 He is also the author of the blog: www.bradfordmuslim.blogspot.com

Others say that segregation is less deliberate and is more often the result of economics. Nisha Kapoor, a specialist in integration at the University of Manchester, says:

"Concentrations of ethnic minorities have grown for demographic reasons due to younger population structures than [among] the majority white population … Analysis of migration trends show dispersal into white areas; self-segregation is a myth."

Whatever the cause, the concentration of ethnic minorities – and particularly South Asians – in particular districts can have important consequences for many women. Ghazala Khan, the project manager of Naye Subah, a mental health-orientated charity and advice centre in Bradford, says:

"The problem is bigger here because we get more segregation in the North than in the South. Asian women's refuges operate here but they are all undercover and don't operate in the freedom they get in London."

Ila Patel, director of the Asha Project, a refuge in Streatham in South London, says that women who are referred to them from towns in northern England are often more afraid of their families and have a strong sense of being part of a community whose members keep them under close surveillance:

Shahien Taj, the director of the Henna Foundation in Cardiff, says:

"The residents we have who come from the North are usually more terrified of being found. Up North the communities are smaller and they know each other; they are tighter."

66 Arab women have a greater understanding of their rights than their South Asian counterparts. They can also understand the interpretations of the Quran so they know their rights. They also have cultural baggage but it not as visible as the people that came from the [Sub] continent. But when things go wrong, it is no different to the Pakistani and the Bangladeshi community 99

In addition, the development of highly-segregated areas has, in some cases, caused communities to become even more isolated and less willing to take advice from people who are not part of their cultural, ethnic or religious group. Shaminder Ubhi, director of the Ashiana Women's Refuge in Leyton in East London, says that this may have an impact on the government's ability to influence such communities:

"What we find is that perhaps interventions from people outside of the community are not that well received, because sometimes it can be seen as intrusive, and 'what the hell are you doing here' and 'what do you know about our community' as a state or the police or government … there is a bit of a resistance."

One result of this, according to Ubhi, is that, in many cases, only Asian individuals and groups can influence Asian communities. She says:

"I think it is easier for us to go into the communities and speak to them as a local Asian women's group, and talk about the issues and how they are affecting women and begin that dialogue and debate. But there is also a resistance when you've got certain community leaders who say 'it doesn't happen in our communities' and who say what we are doing is 'breaking up families'."

These problems may be becoming even more acute in harder-to-reach immigrant communities (Somali or Turkish, for example), who often distance themselves from other immigrant groups as well as from wider society. Yasmin Rehman, deputy lead on honour-based violence at ACPO (Association of Chief Police Officers), says:

Shahien Taj, director of the Henna Foundation, a women's group in Cardiff, says:

66 I don't think that people are actually that intelligent to refer to [Islamic] books; it is a learned behaviour 99

"There's a group called Rights of Women[98] who run a domestic violence helpline in North London. They say that the majority of the calls they receive, month after month, are consistently from the Somali community. There's something going on with them – there's something that we need to look into."

Other women's groups working in highly segregated northern towns say the close-knit nature of some communities can benefit women. In Accrington, Debbie Fawcett, the manager of the Hyndburn and Ribble Valley Outreach women's group which tackles domestic violence with the help of traditional community elders, says:

"On one hand it is a small community and everyone knows everyone. But at the same time once you're accepted by the community leaders and it's clear that they support you, then you're in. The downside of this is that if you upset them then you're out."

Unlike many South Asians, most Arabs in the UK live in London and are often from more urbanised environments in Egypt, Syria and Lebanon. Perhaps as a result, their experiences in the UK can differ significantly from those of other immigrants. Walik Moustafa, an Egyptian-born community activist and doctor in London, says:

"The Asian community is not tied to their mother country as much as Arabs are. The Arabs are tied to their country of origin in a pathological way; the Arab emphasis is that they get in touch with their local community not for support but for political reasons and material gains."

Shahien Taj, director of the Henna Foundation in Cardiff, says:

---

98 www.rightsofwomen.org.uk

"Arabs are a bit more sophisticated about how they do things. The women from my experience are a bit stronger. Also, Arab women have a greater understanding of their rights than their South Asian counterparts. They can also understand the interpretations of the Quran so they know their rights. They also have cultural baggage but it not as visible as the people that came from the subcontinent. But when things go wrong, it is no different to the Pakistani and the Bangladeshi community."

By comparison, the insular nature of many Kurdish immigrant communities has slowed down the spread of new ideas and has led directly to the honour killings of several Kurdish women. Heshu Yones, for example, was killed by her father after his Kurdish co-workers told him that she had been seen behaving "like a prostitute" by dating a Christian and acting in a 'western' manner.[99]

■ Islamist groups

Many Islamist groups encourage violence against women by promoting traditional ideas of honour as well as modern Islamist ideas which say that the health of a Muslim society is dependent on the chastity and sexual fidelity of its females.

Islam is rarely directly cited as a cause of honour-based violence either by witnesses, victims or perpetrators. At the same time, however, it is clear that some current understandings of Islam – however vaguely held – can play a central role in legitimising violence against women and sustaining traditional values. Shahien Taj, director of the Henna Foundation, a women's group in Cardiff, says:

"I don't think that people are actually that intelligent to refer to [Islamic] books; it is a learned behaviour. People might have come across it, but it is usually vague ambiguous statements that they use from years ago; passed through the grapevine."

Members of British Islamist groups frequently direct much of their anger against independent and self-sufficient women whom they can often regard as agents of 'westernisation'. 'Ibn Qazi', a former member of al-Muhajiroun and Hizb ut-Tahrir (HT) from South East London who is of Pakistani origin, says:

"With more intellectual groups like HT, women are encouraged to be active and take more of a proactive role in their community and

99 *The Observer*: 'Death before dishonour' by Geraldine Bedell. 21 November 2004. http://www.guardian.co.uk/gender/story/0,11812,1356386,00.html

sometimes they are the ones on the front line organising events and conferences for the groups. I don't think that members of HT would ever encourage violence against women or be affected by honour as they themselves rebelled from their parents' perspective on life.

"However, if you look at off-shoot organisations like al-Muhajiroun with their immature agendas, women are forced to take the back seat as restrictions through their perceptions of religious teachings are imposed. They are told to cover up, not to work and, if in a job, they are told to leave that job; they are pulled out of education. These women themselves believe that it is their religious duty to stay at home, not to mix with 'western' public and men, not to go to school and not to work. Violence is also encouraged to be used if these women break any of those restrictions.

"Also, during their heyday, such groups would also picket heavily populated Muslim neighbourhoods, and their main focus would be to target women in the community if they were known to have a boyfriend and for not covering up. They would get singled out and ridiculed in the high street in front of the public. They would say threatening things, and on some occasion it got physical, where a hijab is forced on a girl. They would literally terrorize the community."

Gina Khan, a woman's rights activist, who had to flee her home town of Birmingham after recieveng threats from Islamists, believes that the problem lies with specific a interpretation of Islam. She says:

"Wahhabi teachings are being pumped into people's homes through Islamic TV stations and radio and people are falling for it. The Jihadi ideology which is being taught oppresses women and if they managed to create an Islamic state the first thing they would do is to reverse the rights of women."

Nazir Afzal, the Crown Prosecution Service's lead on honour-based violence who also works on terrorism cases, says:

"If you had a map of the UK showing the location of Islamist groups – or terrorist cells – and you had another map showing the incidence of honour-based violence and you overlaid them you would find that they were a mirror; they would be almost identical. It could be that this is simply because this is where South Asians live or it could be something else – it could suggest that there is a strong link between these two attitudes."

Many women's groups say Islamist groups play a key role in defending conservative views towards women. An outreach worker from a women's group in one Northern town – who did not

'Ibn Qazi', a former member of al-Muhajiroun and Hizb ut-Tahrir from South-East London who is of Pakistani origin, says:

66 [In] organisations like al-Muhajiroun with their immature agendas, women are forced to take the back seat as restrictions through their perceptions of religious teachings are imposed. They are told to cover up, not to work and, if in a job, they are told to leave that job; they are pulled out of education. These women themselves believe that it is their religious duty to stay at home, not to mix with the western public and men, not to go to school and not to work. Violence is also encouraged to be used if these women break any of those restrictions 99

ISLAMISTS AND HONOUR

Islamist groups and individuals frequently link ideas of honour with the welfare of the Muslim world. By using words such as Ird and Namus in a political context, they imply that by protecting the chastity of Muslim women, the security and collective honour of Islam and Muslim states and individuals can also be defended. This politicisation of women's bodies helps create an environment where the abuse and control of women is tolerated.

Namus: The word *namus*, used to denote sexual honour in countries such as Turkey, Iran and Kurdistan, has been used extensively by Islamists (and nationalists) to mobilize their supporters against foreign influences and ideas.

In the 19th and early 20th centuries, the word was used by Iranian nationalists to build a stronger national identity. By portraying the vatan, the homeland, as a female; comforting and motherly but in need of protection, they argued that forcefully defending the namus-i-Iran was an obligation for all Iranians.[1]

Since the 1990s, propaganda produced by Chechen rebels has similarly used the idea of namus to rally Turkish volunteers to their jihad which they portrayed as an effort to defend the collective ethno-religious namus of Chechnya and, by extension, of the Muslim world. This appeal to a person's namus operates of a number of levels, appealing to a community's sexual jealousy through stories of Muslim women being raped by Russian soldiers as well as to a sense of machismo associated with defending one's homeland which is in turn portrayed as female.[2]

Ird: In the 1980s Abdullah Azzam, Osama bin Laden's mentor, used ird to inspire Arab Muslims to join the jihad against Soviet troops in Afghanistan. Seeking to appeal to Muslim men, Azzam wrote in Jihad Shaab Muslim, "How can we [Muslims] have moral laws that make the feeding of the hungry if capable, yet we sit by and see the Soviets attack the ird of the Afghans".[3] During the 1980s, Hassan al-Turabi, the leader of the Muslim Brotherhood in Sudan, enforced Sharia laws saying that they would protect the ird of women.[4] Osama bin Laden has also made extensive use of sexualized ideas of honour to justify al-Qaeda's actions, depicting western involvement in the Middle East as an insult against the honour of Arabic men. In 1998 he told Al-Jazeera that the stationing of US troops in Saudi Arabia was an assault on the collective honour of the Arab and Muslim world: "We believe that we are men, Muslim men who must have the honour of defending [Mecca]. We do not want American women soldiers defending [it].... The rulers in that region have been deprived of their manhood. And they think that the people are women. By God, Muslim women refuse to be defended by these American and Jewish prostitutes".[5]

---

1 Afsaneh Najmabadi 'The Erotic Vatan [Homeland] as Beloved and Mother: To Love, to Possess, and To Protect' in *Comparative Studies in Society and History*, Vol. 39, No. 3 (Jul., 1997), (page 442-467)

2 Brian Glyn Williams and Feyza Altindag 'Turkish Volunteers in Chechnya' in *Jamestown Terrorism Monitor*, Volume 3, Issue 7 (April 07, 2005) http://www.jamestown.org/terrorism/news/article.php?articleid=2369571

3 *The Late Sheikh Abdullah Azzam's Books* by Youssef Aboul Enein (The Combatting Terrorism Center, West Point)

4 *Revolutionary Sudan: Hasan Al-Turabi and the Islamist State, 1989-2000* by J. Millard Burr, Robert Oakley Collins (Brill, 2003) (page 21)

5 'America and the War' By Tony Judt in *The New York Review of Books* (Volume 48, Number 18, November 15, 2001)

wish to be named for fear of reprisals – said that some Muslim men there had formed a group to attempt to intimidate female activists which they felt were undermining the image of Asians by publicising domestic violence. She says:

> "We got challenged by a young group called Young Professional Asian Workers, who are mainly Pakistani males. They said that forced marriage and honour-based domestic violence does not exist in our society. And that group also worked for the mosque leaders."

In some cases, campaigns by Islamists have successfully silenced women who speak out against religiously-justified violence against women. Gina Khan, a woman of Pakistani origin living in Birmingham at the time, was the target of a campaign of intimidation against her and her children after she publicly denounced local Islamists' teachings on women. As a result she was forced to halt her campaigning and flee with her children to another part of the UK where she now lives in hiding. She says:

> "It was horrible, the first I heard of it was when my daughter came home one night and started telling me that there are a lot of nasty men out there who are talking about us to other people and who also said a few things to her. Then the local imam would show up and ask if I wanted to send my daughters to a madrasa. He came a few times, but how did he know where I was living, I was surrounded by two white neighbours and didn't mix much with the community. Then I started getting silent phone calls with the odd deep breathing. Then one night, middle of the night a brick came crashing in through the sitting room window while we were sleeping. After a while I decided that it was not safe anymore and I had to leave."

As a response to such intimidation, many women's groups have adapted their outreach methods to continue to reach vulnerable women. Ghazala Razzaq, centre co-ordinator at Roshni Asian Women's Resource Centre in Sheffield, says:

> "We can't be seen as going out there telling people to stop doing what they are doing. We act under a guise; we bring the women in first, then educate them on what is tolerable and not. If we are just a group that deals with getting women away from violent relationships or fleeing forced marriage, then our success rate will be much lower because they wouldn't come. It works better if we are in the community empowering women."

■ *Community and religious leaders*

Among many South Asian, African and Middle Eastern immigrants, 'community leaders' and clerics play a key role in shaping the ideas and values held by those communities in the UK. In many cases, such leaders – who are almost always men – forcefully uphold and defend conservative ideas of honour on other communities.

Community leaders can hold official positions in religious institutions or in local community groups. Alternatively, they can be people who hold land and/or power 'back home' and hence have status and influence among immigrants in the UK. In many cases, these community leaders are highly reluctant to admit that their community has any problem with honour-based domestic violence.

Nazir Afzal, the Crown Prosecution Service lead on honour crimes, says:

> "When you talk to community leaders there are basically two responses. The first response is that they say there is no problem; that they deny that anything is wrong. The second response is that they don't deny it and they acknowledge it as a problem but they then say that they have other priorities instead – they just see it as something that is not important to address."

In some communities, community leaders can also be religious leaders. Gona Saed, director of the Middle East Centre for Women's Rights in Peckham in South London, says:

> "Me and Sawsan [Selim, co-ordinator of the Kurdish Refugee Women's Association] have tried to go to mosques to talk about this. And they have said to us 'go away, there is no violence here', 'go away' and 'don't come back'."

Nazir Afzal, the lead for honour-based violence at the Crown Prosecution Service, says:

❝ I tried to get an imam at a previous Eid to talk about this issue to his congregation. He just said that he couldn't. He said that he was paid by his congregation and that his job depended on these people – he said 'they pay my salary – how am I supposed to tell them something that they don't want to hear?' ❞

Typical of such community elders is Sheikh Haitham al-Haddad, an imam of Palestinian origin, educated in Saudi Arabia, who sits on the UK Islamic Sharia Council and is also its spokesman. When asked about forced marriage, al-Haddad says:

> "Forced marriage is a media exaggeration, designed to criticise Muslims and demonise them in this current climate of fear and Islamophobia. There are forced marriages and forced relations in every society and we need to look at the scale of the problem because I believe in a 'western' non-Muslim society there are a lot of forced relationships and domestic violence. There is also the case of rape and forced sex within 'western' culture; also date rape and the list is endless. Again, domestic violence is always shown by the media to be a problem associated with Muslim women; it's not."

When religious and community leaders deny that domestic violence exists in their community, they do not necessarily support violence against women. Instead, they are often reluctant to see the failings of their community aired publicly and their traditions attacked and ridiculed by wider society. This attitude may be more prevalent in some northern areas where the British National Party (BNP) have used reports of honour killings and the well-documented Asian grooming of white girls for sex and prostitution to win support.[100] One women's worker in northern England, who requested anonymity, said:

> "It's about the community cohesion agenda; they [Islamic leaders] want to develop the relationship of the mosque, they are not willing to say anything that is going to rock the boat. So they don't want to mention it because they want to be accepted by the wider community."

The problem is often made worse because many religious leaders are directly funded by their congregations. This can make them reluctant to raise difficult or controversial issues. Nazir Afzal, the lead for honour-based violence at the Crown Prosecution Service, says:

> "I tried to get an imam at a previous Eid to talk about this issue to his congregation. He just said that he couldn't. He said that he was paid by his congregation and that his job depended on these people – he said 'they pay my salary – how am I supposed to tell them something that they don't want to hear'."

Some Muslim groups such as the Muslim Public Affairs Committee UK (MPACUK) have said such problems can be tackled by reforming mosques and replacing foreign-born imams with ones who have been brought up and trained in the UK. Catherine Hossain, an MPACUK campaign manager, says:

> "Mosques are the grass-roots institutions of the Muslim community, and have enormous potential to support the positive development of society. Currently too many mosques simply function as prayer-halls for Muslim men, rather than fulfilling their wider social function. More sermons and Islamic teaching in mosques need to address problems such as the attitude of some men against women. Imams with fluent English and understanding of our society are equipped to tackle these problems. Mosques should also be an accessible source of social support to women suffering domestic violence."

Sheikh Haitham al-Haddad, a Saudi-trained imam based at the al-Muntada al-Islami (The Islamic Centre) who is also the UK Islamic Sharia Council's spokesperson, says:

66 There is no proof that an imam from abroad is going to preach violence against women. If you look at the ones who we have been told have said something or the imams the media mis-quoted – they were either from here or converts 99

---

100 See, for example, *The Sunday Times*, 'Mothers of Prevention' by Julie Bindel. 20 September 2007 http://www.timesonline.co.uk/tol/news/uk/crime/article2538090.ece, Also *The Guardian*: 'Mother out to seize stronghold of 'unforgivable' BNP' by Matthew Taylor. 23 March 2006 http://politics.guardian.co.uk/farright/story/0,,1737567,00.html

Many of those who work to end violence against women agree. Mohamed Baleela, a team leader at the Domestic Violence Intervention Project in Hammersmith West London, says:

> "We need people who are in touch with the issues. How is a cleric who has arrived from Saudi Arabia or Egypt going to advise a 17-year old who was born here? They don't even know that violence against the family is illegal here; that it is a criminal offence. They don't even know that. They keep saying 'well, back home it's not like this'. Well, they're not 'back home' – they're here."

There is, however, evidence that training British-born imams will not, in itself, resolve this problem. Zalkha Ahmed, director of Apna Haq, a women's group in Rotherham, says:

> "British-born imams, they themselves can be violent. In Rotherham we have six mosques and six imams, and we can name those who are violent ... We have a couple of imams from India and their thinking has been clearer. So we can meet a modern imam, who has clear and positive thinking [on other issues] but he can still be a perpetrator."

Conservative religious leaders themselves say there is no reason why British-born imams will be more opposed to domestic violence than imams from abroad. Sheikh Haitham al-Haddad, a Saudi-trained imam based at the al-Muntada al-Islami (The Islamic Centre) in West London who is also the UK Islamic Sharia Council's spokesperson, says:

> "There is no proof that an imam from abroad is going to preach violence against women. If you look at the ones who we have been told have said something or the imams the media mis-quoted – they were either from here or converts. Riyadh ul-Haq;[101] he was born here and was found to be advocating almost everything and looked to attract people to crime."

Catherine Hossain, an MPACUK campaign manager, says:

❝ Mosques are the grass-roots institutions of the Muslim community, and have enormous potential to support the positive development of society ❞

In some cases, community leaders have themselves attempted to carry out honour killings. In 2001 Mohammed Arshad, a Pakistani living in Dundee in Scotland, attempted to have his daughter's husband murdered for marrying her without his permission. Arshad was a founder member of Tayside Racial Equality Commission, chairman of the Tayside Islamic Council, chairman of the Dundee Mosque[102] and an advisor on spiritual and pastoral care

101 Riyadh ul-Haq is a prominent Deobandi preacher educated in northern England. *The Times*: 'The homegrown cleric who loathes the British' by Andrew Norfolk 7 September 2007 http://www.timesonline.co.uk/tol/news/uk/article2402998.ece

102 *The Courier*: '"Hitman" tells court of threat to kill daughter' by Alan Wilson. 5 November 2003. Source: http://www.thecourier.co.uk/output/2003/11/05/newsstory5319672t0.asp

to the Tayside NHS.[103] After his conviction, the Tayside Islamic and Cultural Education Society appealed for his seven-year sentence for incitement to murder to be reduced to community service, presenting a petition signed by 150 people to the court.[104]

The petition read:

> "We the undersigned members of the Muslim community know Mohammed Arshad for many years. And have the highest regards for him. Therefore ask the court to show mercy to him. Mohammed Arshad is a very highly respected and honoured member of the communities. Therefore his attendance is highly required we the above society request his sentence to be re-considered as community work." [sic][105]

Even if community leaders attempt to tackle domestic violence, they may still face opposition from other community members. Shaheen Rasul, the co-ordinator of the Saffer Project, a woman's group belonging to the traditionalist Pakistani Women's Association in the town of Batley south of leeds, says:

> "We've had domestic violence groups and Lifeline come here. We've got them to bring an Asian worker to speak to the Asian community. We've had some parents who found it inappropriate – they didn't want to sit there and listen to these things."

Similar situations occur when community leaders try to help younger generations brought up in the UK while also retaining the trust of older generations. In Lancashire, John Paton, the manager of the Lancashire Family Mediation Service, was approached by an imam from Accrington who said he was unable to help young men and women brought up in a 'western' environment. Paton says:

> "The background to this is that in their area there are a lot of third generation Muslims who are no longer accepting the cultural norms of their parents. However, there are also issues around alcohol and drugs which families are aware of. They take these issues to the imam and he will try to resolve them. But he wasn't able to do so – they weren't listening to him, to put it bluntly. He then approached domestic violence workers in Accrington for help and that's how I got involved."

Kubir Randhawa from the Asian Family Counseling Service in West London which arbitrates in family disputes, says:

66 We are seeing more people now because they are more aware. In the past people used to go to their parents or community elders. Now they are less willing to go to them and try and seek help by contacting someone from the outside. And it is mainly the younger generation that comes to us 99

---

103 2004 Annual report of Spiritual Care Sub-Committee of Tayside NHS board http://www.nhstayside.scot.nhs.uk/about_nhstay/commitees/archive/21_scsc/030505/43520.pdf

104 *BBC*: '"Honour Killing" appeal refused'. 28 July 2006. http://news.bbc.co.uk/1/hi/scotland/tayside_and_central/5224106.stm

105 Appeal Court, High Court of Justiciary (Appeal No: XC1282/03) 28 July 2006 http://www.scotcourts.gov.uk/opinions/2006HCJAC57.html

One consequence of community leaders not speaking out against honour-based violence is that many young people of South Asian or Middle Eastern origin brought up in the UK are afraid to approach them for help. Many would rather approach women's groups. Kubir Randhawa, director of the Asian Family Counselling Service in West London, which arbitrates in family disputes, says:

> "We are seeing more people now because they are more aware. In the past people used to go to their parents or community elders. Now they are less willing to go to them and try and seek help by contacting someone from the outside. And it is mainly the younger generation that comes to us."

Some women's groups say that police and local authorities can sometimes unwittingly reinforce traditional attitudes when they only approach communities through community and religious leaders. Diana Nammi, director of the Iranian and Kurdish Women's Rights Organisation (IKWRO) in East London, says:

> "Many times the police say that the community doesn't want to speak – but that's not the case. There are a lot of people who want to help but the police don't know how to reach them. The police need better links with people rather than always going through the mosques. How are you going to solve the problem if you go through the mosques? The mosques are the source of these backward ideas."

Some of those experienced in tackling honour-based violence say the concept of dealing with groups through 'community leaders' should be rejected entirely. Philip Balmforth, vulnerable persons' officer (Asian women) for the Bradford Police, says:

> "There is no such thing as a 'community leader'. People should not use such words as community leader. I could take you down any street in Bradford and we can find two or three people in any street who say that they are the community leaders. It is all self-appointed; no one has actually voted or elected them. I refer to such people within the Asian community as influential rather than call them community leaders. Because if we call them leaders then that just helps them stay on the top of a pedestal."

In many cases, however, government policy – at both a local and national level – remains based around working through such 'community leaders' rather than directly with individual members of immigrant communities.

Philip Balmforth, vulnerable persons' officer (Asian women) for the Bradford Police, says:

❝ There is no such thing as a 'community leader'. People should not use such words as community leader. I could take you down any street in Bradford and we can find two or three people in any street who say that they are the community leaders. It is all self-appointed; no one has actually voted or elected them ❞

Deterrents to women fleeing abuse

■ *Women being tracked down by community based groups*

Almost all refuges dealing with Asian women report on the existence of informal networks which exist to track down and punish – with death if necessary – women who are perceived as bringing shame on their family and community.

In many cases, women fleeing domestic violence or forced marriages have been deliberately returned to their homes or betrayed to their families by policemen, councillors and civil servants of immigrant origin.

In many areas, women's groups point to particular problems with local taxi firms. Jasvinder Sanghera, the director of the Karma Nirvana refuge in Derby, says:

"We have a huge problem with the taxi drivers here. We just can't trust them. This can be a matter of life and death for these girls. If they get in the wrong taxi, they might just take them straight back home; straight back to the place that they've just escaped from."

'Saamiya', a 16-year old girl who is living in a refuge in northern England after leaving home when her family threatened to kill her after refusing a forced marriage, says:

"When I asked the taxi driver to drop me here, he just asked me 'where are you from', 'who's your dad – does he know you're here?' ... All the Asian community knows about the taxi-firms – it's like a network. There's always someone who's got a friend there who knows your dad."

Sana Bukhari, an outreach worker at Ashiana refuge in Sheffield, says:

"We don't house girls in the refuge anymore, instead we house them with the local housing association because if their families are looking for them then all they have to do is roll up to the train station and ask the taxi drivers who will bring them straight here. All the taxi drivers know where we are and bring people looking for girls straight here."

Although, this practice of exploiting networks originated in many smaller towns, particularly in the Midlands and northern England, it is now becoming increasingly common elsewhere. Lesley Musa, the director of Women's Aid in Glasgow, says:

"This is something new that the community organises such networks

'Saamiya', a 16-year old girl who is living in a refuge in northern England after her family threatened to kill her, says:

❝ When I asked the taxi driver to drop me here, he just asked me 'where are you from', 'who's your dad – does he know you're here? ... All the Asian community knows about the taxi-firms – it's like a network. There's always someone who's got a friend there who knows your dad ❞

and it is becoming more frequent where women are tracked and news is reported. Women who work here believe that it is a common occurrence. It has happened for us and women don't get into taxis in fear of being tracked down."

In many towns, this problem has become so severe that Asian women's refuges have stopped using Asian taxi firms altogether. Imran Rehmen, a support worker at Karma Nirvana in Derby, says:

"We never go with an Asian taxi firm because they might be family or friends of the family."

In other instances, women have been tracked down through family members working in Job Centres accessing their National Insurance (NI) data which indicate where they are collecting their benefits. The Asha Project in Streatham recorded one case when an 18-year old Pakistani Muslim woman was almost abducted from a Job Centre as she went to sign-on after her relatives accessed confidential National Insurance information. Ila Patel, director of the Asha Project in South London, says:

"She went to sign on, and the family was there, and abducted her. Luckily her boyfriend was there and immediately alerted the police."

In other cases women have been tracked through community members accessing details of their mobile phones. Lesley Musa, the director of Women's Aid in Glasgow, says:

Olivia Madden, client co-ordinator for Panah refuge in Newcastle, says:

66 Emotionally, girls escaping forced marriage are confused and upset. As a consequence of running away, they don't go to school, they don't live with their family and they leave their friends. They suffer from stress, depression and anxiety. They are also scared of being in danger and often they are worried about being found out 99

"My colleagues say it is very common for women to be tracked via the use of their mobile phones. They use websites and other devices to track down women. We have had service users who have been chased down through their telephone on many occasions."

Diana Nammi, the director of IKWRO, says similar situations occur within the Kurdish community in North London:

"We have a case where we moved a girl from eight refuges and still her husband found her – even though she had changed her identity. He found her through her National Insurance number. There are people in the council and in government offices who help communities find girls who have gone missing. Leaking confidential information from state organisations is quite common."

Sawsan Selim, the co-ordinator of the Kurdish Refugee Women's Association in North London, says:

"In one case we moved a girl 16 times and always the husband found

95

her. Sometimes we think it happens because they can pay people working in a council or in a bank for information. The problem is that it gives you always a feeling that you are not safe."

Some refuges report that women have been tracked down by bounty hunters, who in some cases, may double as hired killers. In 2006 a Scottish court found Mohammed Arshad, a 51-year old Pakistani Muslim living in Dundee, guilty of trying to hire a hitman to kill a man who had married his daughter without permission. Arshad had offered to pay £1,000 for the murder of his son-in-law, Abdullah Yasin, and to attack and injure two members of his family.[106]

In some cases, the Islamic Sharia Council has disclosed the location of women to their husbands after being approached by refuges to grant the women a divorce. Grace Busuttil, the manager of the North Kirlees Refuge near Leeds, says:

> "We've had an application for divorce go through the Sharia Council which led to the husband finding the wife. He had no idea where she was until he contacted the Sharia Council. Then a week later he knew exactly where she was."

Support workers in women's refuges say that because many women know they can be tracked down if they flee home, this can discourage them from leaving abusive households. They also say that women in refuges can often struggle to recover emotionally from violence because they continue to live in fear of their families. Olivia Madden, client co-ordinator for Panah refuge in Newcastle, says:

> "Emotionally, girls escaping forced marriage are confused and upset. As a consequence of running away, they don't go to school, they don't live with their family and they leave their friends. They suffer from stress, depression and anxiety. They are also scared of being in danger and often they are worried about being found out."

This study has not found any instances of prosecutions being brought against those who have leaked or accessed confidential information which has then been used to commit honour-based violence against women.

Philip Balmforth, vulnerable persons' officer (Asian women) for the Bradford police, says:

66 Due to the nature of my work I have been at risk on numerous occasions. I have been attacked five times, only once it went to court, and that was when it was really serious, the man pleaded guilty and he was charged with affray. That was over me helping his 16-year-old daughter 99

---

106 Appeal Court, High Court of Justiciary (Appeal No: XC1282/03) 8 March 2006 http://www.scotcourts.gov.uk/opinions/2006HCJAC28.html and Appeal Court, High Court of Justiciary (Appeal No: XC1282/03) 28 July 2006 http://www.scotcourts.gov.uk/opinions/2006HCJAC57.html

■ *Violence and threats against women's groups and refuges*

Mohamed Baleela, a team leader at the Domestic Violence Intervention Project in Hammersmith in West London, says:

66 Last time I talked about marital rape in a mosque I nearly got beaten up. Because we said that the law makes it illegal to rape your wife, someone got up and hit me because he was ignorant of the law 99

Many women's refuges report that members of local communities have sought to intimidate their employees in an attempt to force them to reduce or end their activities. In many cases, this has led to refuges having to move away from areas with a high immigrant population or to take measures to protect themselves against violence.

The Karma Nirvana refuge in Derby, based in the heart of the city's immigrant area on Normanton Road, say that they have frequently been the target of abuse. Jasvinder Sanghera, the centre's director, says:

"I had a serious threat this year. I was told by the Sikh community not to help the government or the police. They also told me that I should look out for devices under my car."

Shazia Qayum, who works with Jasvinder Sanghera at Karma Nirvana in Derby, said:

"The communities don't support us. They say that we're women without shame. I've had texts saying that I'm a disgrace to the Asian community; saying I'd better watch my back or I'll get my head chopped off; saying I'm a slut. We've got police boxes in our office that can set off an alarm. I've got a police alarm box in my house – so does Jasvinder. We've had faeces smeared on our windows. I've not had any support from any community leaders."

Fear of violence often means that women's groups cannot base themselves in the heart of immigrant areas. Gona Saed, from the Middle East Centre for Women's Rights, says that although the group mainly focuses on Kurds and Arabs, it has been obliged to work from Peckham, a mainly Black and Afro-Caribbean area of South London, rather than from parts of West London with a much larger Middle Eastern community. Saed says:

"We've thought of going to an area near Edgware Road where there are huge numbers of Arabs … but we have to consider our safety. We have to ask if we really want to be directly in the heart of the community … maybe it's better to stand back and let people come to us."

In many parts of the Midlands and the North, support workers in some women's groups are so afraid of a backlash from the local community that they were unwilling to allow their names to be used in this report. One women's group in the Midlands who wished to remain anonymous says:

"We would not like people to know where we work because of the way they perceive groups like ours. Being Asian, they don't think working in a refuge is a good thing as they see us as home wreckers. It is also for our safety, especially if we live within the community. We empower women, and that is something they are not happy with."

Mohamed Baleela, a team leader at the Domestic Violence Intervention Project in Hammersmith in West London, says:

"Last time I talked about marital rape in a mosque I nearly got beaten up. Because we said that the law makes it illegal to rape your wife, someone got up and hit me because he was ignorant of the law."

On occasion, members of the police service have themselves been attacked by families when they tried to intervene to halt violence towards women. Philip Balmforth, vulnerable persons' officer (Asian women) for the Bradford police, says:

"Due to the nature of my work I have been at risk on numerous occasions. I have been attacked five times, only once it went to court, and that was when it was really serious, the man pleaded guilty and he was charged with affray. That was over me helping his 16-year-old daughter."

The threat of violence against those who work in women's refuges often prevents them operating openly, speaking freely or basing themselves in the heart of their target communities. This means that many women at risk of honour-based violence – particularly those who do not speak English, who are not given money by their husbands or who are not allowed outside the home – find it harder to access services offered by such groups and are often unaware of what help is available to them.

Shazia Qayum, a team leader at Karma Nirvana, in Derby, says:

66 The communities don't support us. They say that we're women without shame. I've had texts saying that I'm a disgrace to the Asian community; saying I'd better watch my back or I'll get my head chopped off; saying I'm a slut. We've got police boxes in our office that can set off an alarm. I've got a police box in my house – so does Jasvinder. We've had faeces smeared on our windows. I've not had any support from any community leaders 99

Difficulties of getting religious divorces

Many women from the Muslim and Sikh communities report that they have difficulties gaining religious divorces from their respective religious leaders. In many cases, this has helped prevent women from these communities from leaving abusive relationships.

■ Islamic marriages

Muslim women are often unable to escape domestic violence or abusive partners because imams are unwilling to allow them to initiate divorces.

Islamic marriages are sometimes carried out in mosques in addition to – or instead of – a civil marriage. Although they have no legal standing in the UK, these Islamic marriages are seen as virtually obligatory for Muslims. Sheikh Haitham al-Haddad, one of the judges on the UK Islamic Sharia Council in Leyton in East London, says:

> "It is important to have an Islamic marriage as well as a civil marriage because Islamically people cannot have matrimonial life without an Islamic wedding."

Without an Islamic wedding, communities will regard a couple as 'living in sin' – even if they have had a UK civil marriage – which can lead to them being ostracised from the community or face violence. Rehana Bibi, a domestic violence advisor at Hyndburn and Ribble Valley Outreach in Accrington, says:

> "If you're Asian, the community doesn't see it as necessary to have English marriages – but you have to have an Islamic marriage."

But while numerous laws have made it easier for women to obtain civil divorces on the grounds of domestic violence or sexual abuse, this is not always true for Islamic marriages. In many cases, the woman's family and community will not accept the validity of a civil divorce and will insist on an Islamic divorce. Until this is obtained, the woman risks being socially ostracised by her family, neighbours and religious community. Lesley Musa, the director of Women's Aid in Glasgow, says:

> "Women are ostracised by their community if they don't get an Islamic divorce despite having a civil divorce. I don't have statistics on this but it is a major problem because although they are divorced, they are still tied down."

Mohamed Baleela, a team leader at the Domestic Violence Intervention Project in Hammersmith, says that this situation can leave women in limbo; divorced under civil law but still married in the eyes of the community:

> "In the eyes of English law they are co-habiting, but in the eyes of Islamic law they are married. So if she goes to an English court to ask for a divorce they will say to her 'you are not married anyway.' And if she goes to a Sharia court she will not be allowed to get divorced without her husband's consent. "

Organisations like the Islamic Sharia Council,[107] the largest of

Shazia Qayum, a team leader at Karma Nirvana in Derby, says:

66 We approached schools in Derby to try and get posters up to let children know that there was help available if they wanted it. This was just before the school holidays which is the most critical time because this is when girls will get taken off to Pakistan or Bangladesh to be married. Unfortunately none of the schools would let us put them up because they said it would offend the parents 99

---

107 Islamic Sharia Council website is at http://www.islamic-sharia.org/

99

several 'Sharia Courts' set up to standardise Muslim marriages in the UK, theoretically permit women to initiate divorce proceedings on the grounds of domestic violence. In practice, however, this is rarely the case. Tanisha Jnagel, the community services team leader for Roshni Asian Women's Aid in Nottingham, says:

> "The Sharia Council and organisations like this are meant to provide help – but in our experience that's not always been the case."

She says that, in her experience, the Islamic Sharia Council will tend to try to balance the women's interests against those of her husband, family and extended community. In many cases, this consultative approach can allow community leaders and family to pressure the women to withdraw plans to divorce or to return to abusive husbands. She says:

> "Within the Sharia Council they will approach family members to listen to the wife's side of the story and the husband's side and then use religious texts to approach the question of whether a divorce should be granted. In our experience this isn't going to result in a solution which is fair for the woman."

Community pressure to avoid divorces and keep families together – and particularly to have children growing up in a two-parent family – means that many Islamic leaders are especially reluctant to grant divorces to married women with children. Keeping families together therefore can often take precedence over protecting women from violence. Rahni Binjie, the project manager of Roshni Asian Women's Aid in Nottingham, says:

> "Married women with children will in general be less able to get a [Islamic] divorce – particularly if they have girl children. This is because the community sees the family structure as being of so much importance."

Members of the UK Islamic Sharia Council however say that while they aim to keep families together, they also often act to prevent men from divorcing their wives on the spot – which would lead to even greater hardship. Sheikh Haitham al-Haddad, the imam at al-Muntada al-Islami (The Islamic Centre) and one of the judges on the Islamic Sharia Council in Leyton in East London, says:

> "We encourage a man to wait till the woman has finished her menstrual cycle before issuing the divorce because then he would have time to think it over and not make a rash decision. The point is to keep the family together and not break it up … Also, the man must not have relations with woman [i.e. an affair] when making the decision;

it is not accepted to have relations while making the decision. Also, it is not advised to issue a divorce and leave the women with nothing, often these decisions are made in anger and are made on the spur of the moment. The man has to also issue a clear statement of divorce before it is accepted."

Members of the UK Islamic Sharia Council are themselves under pressure from community members who believe that the council is too liberal and from family members who believe that they will suffer shame if the council grants a divorce to their female relatives or in-laws. Al-Haddad says:

"We get intimidation by men who are not happy that we are issuing a divorce for their wives and this is usually six or seven times a week. This comes from mixed communities. I have been intimidated a lot over the years. At first we try and ignore it, if not then we give them advice that their actions are un-Islamic."

There are allegations that members of the Islamic Sharia Council have only granted women divorces in return for money. Shahien Taj, director of the Henna Foundation, a women's group in Cardiff, says:

"I have had cases where the Sharia Council is asking for money, as much as £250 to issue a divorce. This woman could have three children and be destitute and they have the audacity to ask for money. Some of them are taking advantage and because they are not regulated they get away with lots of stuff. There are people taking advantage of the system. But there are also nice people in there."

The Islamic Sharia Council says that it has never given in to intimidation and that it always delivers judgments which are fair to women.

■ Sikh divorces

Many Sikh religious leaders refuse to accept the concept of civil divorce and also downplay the presence of issues like honour-based crime and domestic violence in their community. This can create problems similar to those which occur in many Muslim communities.

Narinder Matharoo, the general secretary of Sikh Sangat London East temple in Leyton, says:

"We don't recognise divorce and they don't exist in the Sikh community. The Gurdwara [Sikh temple] is a place of bringing families to-

Narinder Matharoo, the general secretary of Sikh Sangat London East temple in Leyton, says:

66 We don't recognise divorce and they don't exist in the Sikh community. The Gurdwara [Sikh temple] is a place of bringing families together and not for breaking them up; it is a place of happiness and not sadness. We encourage people to stay in relationships because divorce is not allowed 99

gether and not for breaking them up; it is a place of happiness and not sadness. We encourage people to stay in relationships because divorce is not allowed."

In practice, however, this apparent intransigence may matter less than in the Muslim community. If Sikh couples cannot obtain a religious divorce, then they get a civil divorce which, although not welcomed by the community, is not seen as invalid. Matharoo says:

"If people divorce then it is a civil divorce and not a religious one."

The process is also simplified because many Sikh marriages have a civil and religious marriage ceremony conducted simultaneously – which rarely happens among Muslims – meaning that the marriage is recognised in UK law. Matharoo says:

"We usually have two people holding the ceremony; a registrar and a priest. The priest just holds the prayer while the two get married according to the laws of the country. However, there is no religious document that says they just got married. "

This lack of documentation can sometimes make women vulnerable to a variety of abuses. Shahien Taj, director of the Henna Foundation in Cardiff, says:

"In the Sikh community their religious weddings are more of a problem because they do not get a document that says they are married. For example, there was this woman who was going through a forced marriage given £80,000 in the shape of gifts and a house. She got married and within just twenty four hours of the Rukhsi [the departure of the bride to the groom's home], she [discovered that her husband was already married to another woman] and ran away. She got nothing. All she got was the shame, because in the eyes in the community she is married, even though he is already married to someone else."

Women in such situations may be disowned by their families and can often risk becoming destitute as a result – particularly if they do not speak English. Similar issues can also occur in the Hindu and Sikh community as the principle of divorce is similarly not always recognised by religious leaders.

Government failures

Many government policies have inadvertently contributed to the perpetuation of honour-based violence. In particular the lack of a national strategy to tackle crimes of honour across the education system, the police force or in local government has allowed many abuses against women to go un-checked or un-monitored.

■ *Local government/schools failures*

Local government could play a key role in tackling honour-based crime. Instead many local authorities are reluctant to involve themselves in the issue and by doing so actively contribute to the perpetuation of honour-based violence.

Many women's groups say branches of local government are un-willing to involve themselves in 'minority issues' for a variety of reasons ranging from a lack of knowledge of the problem to a politically correct reluctance to intervene in minority affairs for fear of accusations of racism or 'Islamophobia'.

In Derby, members of women's groups have asked schools to put up posters produced by the Foreign and Commonwealth Office warning of the threat of forced marriages. All the schools refused – even though they had put up other posters warning of the dangers of drugs and alcohol. Shazia Qayum, team leader at Derby's Karma Nirvana, says:

> "We approached schools in Derby to try and get posters up to let children know that there was help available if they wanted it. This was just before the school holidays which is the most critical time because this is when girls will get taken off to Pakistan or Bangladesh to be married. Unfortunately none of the schools would let us put them up because they said it would offend the parents."

Qayum says that this was not a policy issued by a central authority but rather was a decision made at the discretion of individual head teachers:

> "We approached head teachers and each one independently said they didn't want them. We had just last week a girl from one of these schools who had been forced to marry."

Jasvinder Sanghera, director of Derby's Karma Nirvana refuge, says:

> "Myself and Shazia [Qayum] asked every school in Derby to put up this poster about forced marriages. And every single school refused for fear of upsetting communities. Yet they put up posters on drugs, alcohol … Schools are afraid to raise the issue because they are afraid of communities – and especially the Muslim community – they are afraid of a backlash."

103

Other women's groups around the country – and particularly in the Midlands and the North – have reported that schools are similarly reluctant to raise issues of forced marriage and domestic violence for fear of upsetting parents of immigrant origin. One women's worker from a town in the Midlands who requested anonymity for fear of violence, says:

"In schools with a large Asian population, schools can be afraid to raise the issue because of the local community saying 'you're putting words in our children's mouths'."

This situation means that the sensitivities of families are often being put ahead of the human rights of thousands of young women. Shazia Qayum, team leader at Karma Nirvana, says:

"It's political correctness gone mad."

An additional problem is that social services and local authorities are often unaware of how honour-based communities function. Zalkha Ahmed, director of Apna Haq, a woman's group in the Midlands, says:

"Social services don't know what the issues are. They got confused last week when they had two women with the same name. They would also say, 'why don't you go to a relative' not knowing that because of honour that relative has also turned their back on them. Having that understanding is crucial in areas where specialised groups don't exist."

This problem appears more common in areas where segregation means that white council workers do not often mix informally or socially with people from South Asian backgrounds.

■ Government employees failing to uphold law

Several women's groups say that many South Asians working in local government and the police service abuse their positions to defend traditional practices and to block attempts to halt honour-based violence.

In many northern towns where immigrant communities are tight-knit and conservative, some women's refuges say that South Asian women are often afraid to seek help because they know that many Asians working in local government and in private firms believe that women who break traditional taboos deserve to be punished. John Paton, manager of the Lancashire Family Mediation Service which is based in Preston, says:

John Paton, manager of the Lancashire Family Mediation Service which is based in Preston, says:

66 One issue we have come up against is the issue of confidentiality. It's extremely difficult for an Asian woman to go to a community worker or an agency where she knows that there are potentially people there who will report back to her family what she has said 99

"One issue we have come up against is the issue of confidentiality. It's extremely difficult for an Asian woman to go to a community worker or an agency where she knows that there are potentially people there who will report back to her family what she has said. This goes on to the extent that there is a solicitor's in Blackburn that has no Asians [working there] and as a result of this it receives a very disproportionate amount of business from Asian women. In particular, this solicitors is involved in getting a lot of court injunctions to prevent husbands from seeing their wives. This is contrary to the doctrine which says that agencies should recruit more people from ethnic minorities because Asians want to talk to other Asians – to people who are like themselves. In this particular case it acts against the very interests of the people they are trying to help because it actually may deter Asian women from using these services."

Zalkha Ahmed, director of Apna Haq, a women's support group in the North of England, says some translators working for social services have deliberately blocked government attempts to help South Asian women who are fleeing violence and abuse:

"We have also had translators who would lie to the social services when women go to seek help. The translators would not reveal the extent of the story, and try to play down the extent that honour had to play in the problem to try and portray a positive image of the community."

Ena Mercy, director of the Pennines Domestic Violence group which is based in Huddersfield, home to a large Pakistani and Sikh population, says some councillors there have sought to block the activities of women's groups:

"You get councillors who try to exercise control. You get Asian councillors trying to stop our meetings from happening. Other councillors – white councillors – are afraid of upsetting the Asian councillors and the other community leaders. They're afraid of being called racist or whatever."

Similar incidents reportedly occur in Bradford. The chairperson of a women's project in Bradford, who wishes to remain anonymous because she is concerned for her safety, says:

"We have a lot of pressure from the local councillors in Bradford; they are the bad ones, because they abuse their power by trying to get details on who is staying with us and what they are doing. They give us a hard time, till we have to complain to the police and they back off. They are dominant males who are trying to bully us."

A worker in another woman's refuge in northern England who also requested anonymity for safety reasons says:

A chairperson of a Bradford-based women's group, who wished to remain anonymous because of death threats, says:

66 We have a lot of pressure from the local councillors in Bradford, they are the bad ones, because they abuse their power, by trying to get details on who is staying with us and what they are doing. They give us a hard time, till we have to complain to the police and they back off 99

105

C A S E   S T U D Y

'HAPPY FAMILIES' – A POEM BY SHAFILEA AHMED

In 2003, Shafilea Ahmed, a 17 year old schoolgirl of Pakistani origin, disappeared from her home in Warrington, Cheshire. She had previously tried to kill her herself by drinking bleach in an attempt to avoid being taken back to Pakistan for an arranged marriage Her decomposed body was discovered in a river in Cumbria in February 2004. Although the police have suspected that the girl was the victim of an honour killing, the girl's family have denied murdering their daughter. In the family's home, police discovered a poem apparently written by the girl shortly before her disappearance.

Shafilea's poem in full: 'Happy Families'

> I don't pretend like we're the perfect family no more
> Desire to live is burning
> My stomach is turning
> But all they think about is honour
> I was like a normal teenage kid
> Didn't ask 2 much
> I jus wanted to fit in
> But my culture was different
> Now I'm sitting here
> Playing happy families
> Still crying tears
> But no we're a happy family
> I have these fears
> I wish, I wish, I wish
> For a happy family ----- oh yeah
> I lay in bed hoping the next day would be better
> It was just a thought
> Because it never happened no
> But still I dream of this today yeah hey
> I wish my parents would be proud of wot I done
> Instead it's you've have bought shame
> Or something else lame
> I don't wanna hear this no more
> No no no.
> I feel trapped
> I feel trapped, so stuck I don't wot 2 do the feeling is mutual, I don't know how to explain
> Im a trapped so trapped (so trapped)
> Now u know where I stand, when I fall back I got no where else to land
> I don't know how to say
> I'm trapped so trapped I'm trapped wit u.
> It was my last year in school, so happy with my friends I got lots to do ---
> But came this day when everything changed
> I came home it seemed like a normal day

But sumthing wasn't right ----
I wish I coulda changed the event
I shoulda killed myself instead
I'd rather have been dead
Coz now I have a burden on my chest
And no it won't go away, the guilt, the pain
When I look back on things I coulda changed coulda stop, prevented, exchanged
But i had to turn out this way (so trapped)
Now I'm sitting on my window bay
Looking at the rain ----
Drowning sorrow and pain
Will this ever go away ----
I feel trapped so trapped, I'm trapped
I'm trapped, so trapped I'm trapped
(I don't know wot do) I feel trapped.
But my family ignored

The Asian News 'Were these her final words of despair.' 19 December 2003.
http://www.theasiannews.co.uk/news/s/480/480998_were_these_her_final_words_of_despair.html

"The councillors are interested in votes, and they are usually from a certain family that the community looks up to, so they have to act a certain way."

In some cases, this problem has even reached the judiciary with Asian members of the courts services on occasion acting to protect their community's values. Jasvinder Sanghera, director of the Karma Nirvana refuge in Derby, says:

"Because we're not seen as amenable, to them we are enemies. An Asian woman magistrate has stood up and called me an 'imposter' … The communities don't see us as honourable; they see us as people who are undermining their whole way of life."

■ 'No recourse to public funds' rule

Women who have recently arrived in the UK are often unable to escape violence from their husbands or in-laws because of the 'No Recourse to Public Funds' (NRPF) rule which prevents immigrants from claiming many forms of benefits within two years of arriving in the UK.

Lesley Musa, the director of Women's Aid in Glasgow, says:

"No recourse to public funds is a huge problem. Women tend to

107

THE 'NO RECOURSE TO PUBLIC FUNDS' RULE

The NRPF rule was initially introduced to attempt to stop recent arrived immigrants claiming large amounts of public funds. In its present form the rule prevents immigrants who have been in the UK for less than two years from claiming unemployment benefits, housing allowances, income support and carer allowances among others.

It does allow immigrants access to the National Health Service, education and the emergency services, however. The Domestic Violence Immigration Rule (introduced by the Home Office in 2002) allows women who have arrived in the UK as spouses or partners to apply for residency within their two-year probationary period if they prove that domestic violence had caused their relationship to break down and that they needed to remain in the UK. This law did not grant women in this situation the right to use public funds however. However women with children who leave their partner within two years of arriving in the UK may be entitled to some support under the 1989 Children's Act.

A more comprehensive list of which public funds can and cannot be accessed by recent immigrants is at No Recourse to Public Funds – What Does It Mean?, a guide produced by the Home Office.

Source: "No Recourse to Public Funds" (Leaflet produced by the Home Office). http://www.bia.homeoffice.gov.uk/sitecontent/documents/residency/publicfunds.pdf

be penniless with no access to any money. Usually they don't have money because they have had to escape and don't have a job because of their situation or lack of skill. These women then become reliant on charity and a lot of refuges cant afford to help them."

Women's refuges say that a significant proportion of women who come to them have no recourse to public funds. Shaminder Ubhi, Ashiana's director in Leyton in East London, says:

"We deal with a huge number of women with no recourse to public funds. Only last year [between April 06-March 07] we supported 595 women all together. Under 'no recourse' we saw 80 women and 92 women had immigration issues."

Many women's groups and activists believe that many families often purposely leave the immigration status of their 'imported spouse' in hiatus to exert maximum control over them. This sometimes also occurs to men who can be forced to work for little or no money in the businesses run by their new in-laws.

Jenny Moody, the chairperson of Luton's Women's Aid says:

> "Money can be used for control. Just like women with no recourse to public funds having their passports taken, and if they don't have money then their husbands have complete control."

Women who flee their marital homes to escape violence or abuse within two years of arriving in the UK can become vulnerable to further abuses. Kubir Randhawa, director of the Asian Family Counselling Service in Southall in West London, says:

> "They can't get a job because they don't have a national insurance number; they have no status in this country, so basically they are on their own. Also, people from back home can't actually support them because of the exchange rates, so no matter how many thousand rupees they came into the country with, it's not enough to even last them two days."

The result is that many women are often forced to stay in abusive relationships for fear of becoming destitute. Mohamed Baleela, team leader at the Domestic Violence Intervention Project in Hammersmith in West London, says:

> "A lot of women choose to stay in violent relationships because they have nowhere to go. If they have children, the social services have a duty to help them under government laws. But if they don't have children there are no facilities in place to help them."

This problem is made worse because the No Recourse to Public Funds rule means that refuges usually cannot use government money to help women with unresolved immigration status. Refuges which cannot afford to support women are forced to turn them away. Grace Busuttil, the manager of the North Kirlees Refuge near Leeds, says:

> "I won't accept anyone with 'no recourse to public funds' unless I have it in writing from social services saying that they will support them."

However the level of support given to refuges by local councils varies widely. Some councils provide extensive financial support for women who are affected by the 'No Recourse' rule. Others do not. Ila Patel, director of the Asha Project in Streatham, notes that the borough of Lambeth is not fully supportive of such women. She says:

> "We do get referrals all the time. It also depends on the borough you are in because Islington has a 'no recourse to public funds' network, and things are a lot easier there. So if you are a refuge in Islington the

---

C A S E   S T U D Y

NO RECOURSE TO PUBLIC FUNDING

Rukhsana, 23 – She was married at 18; doesn't speak English. As soon as she left her husband she found that she does not have the support of her family or the community.

I've now been staying in the refuge for four months since I left my husband's home. I don't have a residency, so I don't get money from the government, the only money I get is from the section 16 in Children's Act. Basically, the money I get is for my daughter only.

I am finding life difficult on my own; there is no support from the community or relatives because of honour. These people only offer to help because they want something. During the marriage I was turned away from the community and after the marriage I got no support from them. The power is with the men of the community.

I am under extreme pressure in bringing up my daughter, getting money for us, getting an education and generally all the challenges in life. My daughter now says 'where is my dad?' and 'where is my family?'. It's no life for her to grow up in a refuge.

I would go back to Pakistan, but I want to sort out my residency for my daughter's sake. I don't want her to grow up with the mentality that I grew up in. I don't want her to end up in a marriage like mine. I want what is best for her. And returning back home would be disaster for both of us because we will have no one to turn to and we will be homeless.

The first thing I have to do for my future is to resolve my stay here. Finish my English lessons, get a job and move out. I want to study and work in IT.

I feel helpless and hopeless; there is nothing to keep me going on living apart from my daughter. I want them to suffer. The government needs to do something. I think the government should make the husbands of abandoned spouses' pay for the damage they have caused.

He should be punished for this. Why should me and a child suffer? What did we ever do? I think he [my husband] was a taxi driver – 'don't interfere', he would say when I tried to ask him what he does or where he goes. Even though my in-laws don't want my daughter they are willing to take her in order to get me deported.

No one could ever understand what I am going through – depression, anxiety and not being able to think straight. If I had stayed in Pakistan I would have been able to have gotten an education and make something out of myself. Now I have to battle to survive.

---

local authorities under section 4 and 21 will help. In Lambeth we find that there isn't much help [from the council]."

Philip Balmforth, vulnerable persons' officer (Asian women) for the Bradford Police, says:

"They are very lucky in Bradford; it costs the council £190,000 a year paying out for these women. They will put two to three women together in one house to save money."

110

All women's groups interviewed for this report believe that in its present form, the 'No Recourse to Public Funds' rule has greatly increased the suffering of hundreds of women. Women who are suffering domestic violence are deterred from leaving home. Women who do leave are more likely to become destitute or forced to return to their abusive relationship.

Wrong government partners/advisors

The British government and police largely seek to deal with minorities through intermediaries who, they believe, can manage the community on behalf of the state. In many cases this policy has strengthened the influence of elderly and conservative men who are likely to support traditional ideas of honour and patriarchy – and who are reluctant to condemn violence against women.

■ *Muslim Council of Britain (MCB)*

In dealing with the Muslim community, the government has often worked through the Muslim Council of Britain which describes itself as the "largest umbrella body of Muslim groups in the UK".[108] The MCB has sought to block legislation aimed at ending honour-based violence. Almost all women's groups interviewed for this report say that the MCB has done little or nothing to end honour-based violence against women.

In particular, the MCB has sought to block attempts to criminalise forced marriage, arguing that "a new law on forced marriages will have the real risk of being seen to target ethnic minorities"[109]. Partly as a result of the MCB's pressure, the government halted its plans to criminalise forced marriage and made it a civil offence instead. This reflects what many see as the organisation's lack of interest in women's issues. Nazir Afzal, the Crown Prosecution Service's lead on honour-based violence, says:

> "The MCB pretty much don't want to get involved. They've made it abundantly clear that they believe that the Islamic community has other priorities. They'd rather talk about Islamophobia or anti-terrorism laws instead – they say that these are the things that matter to the

108 The MCB describes its self as this in *Judge Drabu Receives Lifetime Achievement Award From Association Of Muslim Lawyers.* 19 November 2007. http://www.mcb.org.uk/features/ features. php?ann_id=1659

109 *The Muslim Council of Britain (MCB) response to consultation paper 'Forced Marriage – A Wrong not a Right'* 8 December 2007. It is available online at http://www.mcb.org.uk/uploads/wrongnotright.pdf p.2

Muslim community. In fact, the biggest fear that Muslim women have is not Islamophobia or anti-terrorism laws; it's the violence that they face from their own families."

Hassan Safour, a project officer in refugee and integration issues at the Muslim Welfare House in Finsbury Park in North London, says:

"If you ask them a question, the MCB will probably give you the right answer – but whether they're doing enough is a different question. In terms of taking action I'm not sure they're doing much. If there's an honour killing they might condemn it but in terms of taking action I don't see much. I don't think it is one of their priorities."

Contempt for the MCB appears widespread among women's groups. Rafaat Mughal, the director of Joint Association of Nissa Trusts, says:

"The MCB has done nothing. The MCB has failed. I was a member but have withdrawn my membership. First of all they have no women. They are clueless and sexist. They always talk negatives – never positives. I have no faith with them."

In recent months, however, the MCB has begun taking more action to tackle honour-based crime, primarily through Ibrahim Mogra, chair of the Inter Faith Relations committee in the MCB. Shahien Taj, director of the Henna Foundation in Cardiff, says:

"The MCB have done nothing for years but only a few months ago, through Ibrahim Mogra, they have just realised that [honour violence] is a problem. They have been in denial and I have told them that they have been a let-down. They can play a crucial part, but I don't think they have much credibility."

It remains to be seen whether Mogra will be able to exert a significant influence on MCB policy as a whole. The MCB's action on these issues to date have not only hurt Muslim women but women from all honour-based communities.

■ Southall Black Sisters

The government has relied heavily on the Southall Black Sisters for information on honour based violence in the UK. Founded in 1979, this feminist group has campaigned against honour killings and domestic violence, and championed abused women who killed their husbands as well as offering counselling and support to abused women. More recently, however, the group has virtually stopped carrying out grassroots work and

Rafaat Mughal, the director of Joint Association of Nissa Trusts, says:

> 66 The MCB has done nothing. The MCB has failed. I was a member but have withdrawn my membership. First of all they have no women. They are clueless and sexist. They always talk negatives – never positives. I have no faith with them 99

its helpline is rarely answered. In consequence it has lost touch with the community that it aims to serve.

Philip Balmforth, vulnerable persons' officer (Asian women) for the police in Bradford, says:

> "I once said to a police sergeant in Southall that he was lucky to have the Black Sisters there, and he said 'not really, they are never here'; they don't have a hostel or anything. It is two old women sitting in an office, getting good money from the government to criticize the government. My personal point of view is that whenever I have been to a meeting in England, everyone has heard of them but no one has ever spoken to them. It is quite wrong in my opinion that the government should give them money as advisors and they [Southall Black Sisters] don't then consult with other groups around the country. I have been to high powered meetings around the country and you would think some people would have had some sort of documentation, a phone call, or some sort of an email from them just to say 'what do you think of this', but none of that happens."

Humera Khan, the co-founder of An-Nisa Society, a women's advocacy group in Wembley in London, says:

> "I do respect Southall Black Sisters for the work they have done in challenging legislation, [But] they are very unpopular because they are absolutists in their methodology; they don't believe at all in mediation and don't listen and that is a problem. "

Many groups in the Midlands and the North of England also say that government policy is too London-orientated. Jasvinder Sanghera, the director of the Karma Nirvana refuge in Derby, says:

> "I'm constantly having to tell people that the world does not revolve around London. Because Karma Nirvana is outside London we are aware of a lack of engagement with us because the government is in London. In some cases we've had to fight to get into these meeting rooms."

Several women's refuges have also said that the government does not sufficiently take into account how regional variations in segregation, education and employment affect the way in which honour-based violence should be tackled.

Policing failures

In general, women's refuges say the police services are becoming better at tackling honour based violence. Many victims of honour-based violence also say their experiences with the police have been overwhelmingly positive. Many believe that the prompt action taken by individual officers has saved their lives. However, many women's groups also say that police work on honour-based violence is still sometimes hampered by a lack of awareness and specialised training.

Women's groups often say that frontline police officers do not appreciate how quickly honour-based violence can escalate, and consequently, that they may underestimate the risks facing women who have fled their homes. Sawsan Salim, co-ordinator of the Kurdistan Refugee Women's Organisation in North London, says:

> "In the last three months we had six or seven cases which we forwarded to the police and they never replied. For example, on one occasion we had a case where a girl had suffered domestic violence and believed that she might be in danger of an honour killing and she had run away from home. We went with her to the police station at three pm but the policeman said he didn't have enough time to take her statement as he was finishing work at five pm; he said that writing up a case report would take three hours and he had to go home in two hours. We told them it was an emergency and we wanted immediate help, and they did nothing. They need to realise the difference between domestic violence and potential honour crimes; that it's a matter of life and death."

Police failures can have devastating consequences. Several women have been killed by their relatives after the police underestimated the risk they faced from their families. The most high-profile such failure led to the death of Banaz Mahmod, a 20-year old Kurdish woman, in January 2006. Derya Yildirim, a project co-ordinator for Refuge's community outreach project in South London, says:

> "Banaz went to the police and she said that she was scared for her life – but police couldn't comprehend this. And in the case of Heshu [Yones], the education services and social services knew, the police knew. She made a video too. These should have raised alarm-bells but they didn't."

In the weeks leading up to her death, Banaz came to the police at least six times and asked for them to protect her from relatives who wanted to kill her for having an affair outside her arranged

Sawsan Salim, co-ordinator of the Kurdistan Refugee Women's Organisation in North London, says:

66 In the last three months we had six or seven cases which we forwarded to the police and they never replied 99

marriage. On each occasion, the police told her to return home as they believed that she was exaggerating the risks that she faced. Shortly after she approached the police a final time, Banaz was kidnapped by Kurdish men hired by her family, raped repeatedly and then killed. Her body was then chopped up and buried in a suitcase in a garden in Birmingham. Gona Saed, director of the Middle East Centre for Women's Rights in Peckham in South London, says:

> "I am feeling very angry about Banaz's case. At the moment – after the case of Banaz – the police are really making an effort – especially Steve Allen – saying to us 'we want to listen to what you do'. Now they are making a strategy to prevent honour killing. But it's not up to the speed we want it to be. We don't know if it will continue or if after a few months, they will say 'look there are no more honour killings – problem solved'."

Officials involved in tackling honour crimes point to the difficulties of prosecuting everyone who was involved in honour-based violence. Nazir Afzal, the Crown Prosecution Service lead on honour-related violence, says:

> "It's easy to prosecute someone if you've got a knife with blood on it and on the murder weapon you've got the perpetrator's DNA – that's easy. But we have to go after everybody who's involved. It's always much more difficult to go after a conspiracy than to go after a straightforward criminal act."

Some women's groups suggest that specialised teams of police officers who have been specifically trained to recognise and deal with honour killings should be set up. Gona Saed, director of the Middle East Centre for Women's Rights in Peckham in South London, says:

> "Police need to be able to recognise when there is a threat of honour-based violence. The other thing we'd like to see is a special advisory units for the police. We don't expect every policeman to know about honour-based violence but when they suspect something they need to be able to call a specialised unit who can tell them what to do. And at that point they could contact one of these women's organisations – we have a lot of experience and we can tell them what to do."

Several women's groups, particularly in the Midlands and northern England, say they are often reluctant to go to the police with women who have ran away to escape violence because they cannot trust Asian police officers. Zalikha Ahmed, director of the Apna Haq refuge, says:

"We have to be careful with them especially the Asian ones. We don't visit the station when certain Asian officers are on because some of them are perpetrators, and one of them on record said that he would not arrest someone who used force on his wife. Some of them would just expose us for what we do."

Another worker in a women's group in the North, who requested anonymity for safety reasons, said:

"We had instances when a [Asian] chief inspector offered his help to a family by tracking a girl down – we were appalled."

According to some women's groups such problems appear to be practically common in the West Midlands police force. Shahien Taj, director of the Henna Foundation, a women's group in Cardiff, says:

"There have been cases of runaways and women being re-housed where members of the police department have passed on their information to the Asian community network which then tracked down the women. This can also be applied to community leaders and councillors.

"Recently I had a case in Birmingham where a woman was dumped outside a shop at seven pm with her three children. I made calls to a community leader asking for help and he said it was the wrong time of the week and day [Sunday]. A police officer said 'why don't you let me deal with the case?' and the woman said she can't trust the police – because nine times she had run away and nine times the police just returned her to her family where she got abused. On all these occasions the police told the husband where she was, and sent her back to them."

In addition police forces in general are often mistrusted by many ethnic communities. Often this stems from negative experiences with police forces in their countries of origin. Sawsan Salim, co-ordinator of Kurdish Refugee Women's Association in London, says:

"Arab and Kurdish women don't like police, they don't trust them, and it is the same when they come here. Back home the women never trusted police, they were always seen as an oppressing force, police are here to help and women just need to realise that."

Going to the police can also be seen as shameful. While this attitude is common in many South Asian communities, it also applies to other, less high-profile immigrant groups. Saba Melles, an advice worker at Eritrean Community Centre in Islington, says:

Sawsan Salim, co-ordinator of the Kurdistan Refugee Women's Organisation, says:

> 66 Arab and Kurdish women don't like police, they don't trust them, and [it is the same when] they come here. Back home the women never trusted police, they were always seen as an oppressing force, police here are to help and women just [need to] realise that 99

"Even if women come to us about domestic violence, they don't want to report it to the police. You can't force them to report but we can only advise them that this is the best way. They don't want to go to the police because culturally it's not acceptable. Men are always [seen as] the figures of the household and they have the right to treat the family every way they want."

Among many Muslim immigrants this wariness has been heightened by the work of several Muslim pressure groups which have sought to portray the police service as 'Islamophobic'. For instance, the Muslim Council of Britain has said that the 'Stop and Search' powers of London police "were being used unfairly against Muslims".[110] Yvonne Ridley, speaking as an activist for the Respect Party, has similarly told a public meeting in June 2006: "From today until the terrorisation of the Muslim community is stopped immediately, I believe all Muslims should withdraw their support. This goes from asking the community copper for directions to passing the time of day with a beat officer ... We should enforce non-co-operation".[111] Olivia Madden, client co-ordinator for Panah refuge in Newcastle, says:

"This stuff does not help but we tell women to speak no matter to their teachers, doctors and police. We encourage people to speak up and not care about what's in the media or what people are saying. We tell them that the police are here to help and we tell them to talk to them whatever is happening in the background."

In some instances, judges have also passed sentences which seem to indicate that in some cases violence against women by immigrants is acceptable on cultural or religious grounds. For example, in September 2003, Judge Neil Denison sentenced Abdulla Yones to 14 years for murdering his daughter Heshu rather than the recommended 20 years. Denison said that 16-year old Heshu had "provoked" her father by having a Christian boyfriend.[112] In his concluding remarks, he said:

"This is, on any view, a tragic story arising out of irreconcilable cultural differences between traditional Kurdish values and the values of western society".[113]

Saba Melles, an advice worker at the Eritrean Community Centre in Islington, says:

66 Even if women come to us about domestic violence, they don't want to report it to the police 99

110 For example, see the MCB's 'Have Your Say on Police 'Stop and Search' Powers' on Wednesday 6th October 2004 http://mcb.org.uk/features/features.php?ann_id=500

111 *BBC*: 'Call to Muslims over police help'. 7 June 2006. http://news.bbc.co.uk/1/hi/uk/5054600.stm

112 Regina v Abdulla Yones; High Court of Justice, Case No: 2004/659/MTS 20 June 2007 http://www.hmcourts-service.gov.uk/cms/144_12042.htm

113 *The Daily Telegraph*: 'Father gets life for 'honour' killing'. 29 September 2003. http://www.telegraph.co.uk/news/main.jhtml?xml=/news/2003/09/29/ugirl.xml&sSheet=/portal/2003/09/29/ixportaltop.html

Similar cases have occurred in Europe. In early 2007, Christa Datz-Winter, a female judge in Germany, refused to grant a Moroccan woman a divorce on grounds of domestic violence. The judge cited Quranic verses which, she thought, permitted a husband to beat his wife and said that the plaintiff should have known that it was customary for Moroccan husbands to beat their wives.[114]

Summary: Barriers to change

Many observers, particularly those working in northern towns, say that, as a result of the above factors, attitudes have barely changed in two decades. Philip Balmforth, vulnerable persons' officer (Asian women) for the police in Bradford, says:

> "There are no changes with the Asian community; if you came here in 1988 then we would have the same conversation and information that you will get now and next year. Nothing has changed, not a thing, the only thing that has changed is the wider debate about forced marriage and honour-based domestic violence has reached the media."

Nazir Afzal, the lead on honour-based violence at the Crown Prosecution Service, says:

> "I've just about written off this generation. I used to believe that once the older generation have died, all these practices would just die out. But now you get 21 year olds who were brought up here saying exactly the same thing. I had one guy who said to me, 'a man is like a bar of gold, a woman is like a piece of white silk'. He then said that, 'if gold gets dirty you can just wipe it clean, but if a piece of silk gets dirty you can never get it clean again – and you might as well just throw it away'. That's a 21-year old speaking. The work now has to be done with the nine- and ten-year olds.""

Nazir Afzal, from the Crown Prosecution Service, says:

66 I've just about written off this generation. I used to believe that once the older generation have died, all these practices would just die out. But now you get 21 year olds who were brought up here saying exactly the same thing. I had one guy who said to me, 'a man is like a bar of gold, a woman is like a piece of white silk'. He then said that, 'if gold gets dirty you can just wipe it clean, but if a piece of silk gets dirty you can never get it clean again – and you might as well just throw it away'. That's a 21-year old speaking. The work now has to be done with the nine- and ten-year olds 99

---

114 *Der Spiegel*: 'A German Judge Cites Koran in Divorce Case', by Veit Medick and Anna Reimann. 21 March 2007. http://www.spiegel.de/international/germany/0,1518,473017,00.html

CHAPTER 7

Breaking the tradition

Introduction

66 Here in Bradford, [there are] very insular communities who tend to live with each other as family groups, and the same applies in Lancashire. The South is definitely more integrated than the North **99**

Philip Balmforth, vulnerable persons' officer (Asian women) for the Bradford police

Although a culture of honour-based violence is arguably becoming increasingly entrenched in many minority communities in the UK, there are also signs that, in some cases, the strict ideas of honour brought to Britain are starting to erode.

The erosion of traditional values in some communities of immigrant origin is largely due to a mixture of successful government policies, immigrants' increased exposure to other cultures and women's increasing economic independence through enhanced access to education and employment. Examining the factors and processes which are accelerating such changes can provide insights into how the government can act to make such change more likely and widespread.

Many women's groups say that immigrant communities in larger cities are generally proving most receptive to change – even if such progress there remains sporadic. However, evidence from some smaller towns also, on occasion, appears to show that traditional ideas of honour are changing. Ila Patel, director of the Asha Project, a refuge in Streatham in South London, says:

> "My cousin in Leicester can meet friends in a bar and go out with male friends. But in some parts of Wolverhampton that would be totally unacceptable; you just couldn't. The residents we have who come [to the refuge] from the North are usually more terrified of being found. Up North the communities are smaller and they know each other, they are tighter. London and surroundings are more clear and isolated; people don't know each other as much. [Improvements are filtering] from the South to the North but it's very slow ... If I use myself as an example: when I got married, 25-years ago to an English man, I was ostracised from the community so I left as I couldn't deal with the way I was treated. But recently my sister married outside of the community, and it was slightly different; despite people talking about it, she is able to go in and out of the community and she attends community events."

Such changes are not only affecting younger generations but also older people whose own ideas of honour have been gradually challenged by exposure to other cultures and ideas. Ghayasud-din Siddiqui, the head of the London-based Muslim Parliament, says:

> "Even the older people know that there have been so many casualties caused by these practices and even they are starting to feel that something has to be done. Often arranged marriages break down – and because they're between cousins, often relations between brothers also break down. Recently I met a man who said that because of a forced marriage that had gone bad, he was no longer able to talk to his brother. How can anyone see this as a good thing?"

Others point to differences between religious and ethnic groups. Rafaat Mughal, director of the Joint Association of Nissa Trusts in North London, says:

> "Somalis and Hindus are doing very well at the moment; both women are very progressive, especially Somali women. Hindu women are open to ideas and are open [to getting education]. Pakistanis are finally improving and getting a job but mother-in-laws are still a problem in arranged and forced marriages."

In almost all cases, women's groups in the South of the UK report more signs of change than groups in the North. In addition to this, traditional values seem to be changing faster in big cosmopolitan cities such as London, Liverpool and Manchester than in smaller towns, such as Bradford, Luton and Rotherham, where there is a smaller range of immigrant communities and patterns of settlement are more segregated and perhaps more defensive in their response to other cultures. Philip Balmforth, vulnerable persons' officer (Asian women) for the Bradford police, says:

> "When I go to London I see a completely different type of Asian person. I see people who have integrated and want to be part of society who are quite open about the situation. I see them causing little if any problems to anybody in the establishment. Here in Bradford, [there are] very insular communities who tend to live with each other as family groups, and the same applies in Lancashire. The South is definitely more integrated than the North."

Many activists say that the first visible sign of change is often that individuals and communities are becoming willing to critically discuss ideas of honour for the first time. Hassan Safour, project officer in refugee and integration issues at the Muslim Welfare House in Finsbury Park in North London, says:

> "More people are willing to discuss domestic violence than before

Hassan Safour, project officer in refugee and integration issues at the Muslim Welfare House in Finsbury Park in North London, says:

❝ More people are willing to discuss domestic violence than before ❞

CASE STUDY

CHANGING ATTITUDES IN SHEFFIELD

'Rosi' is in her mid 40s and from Mirpur and had been attending the Roshni centre for nine years. Initially she came to the centre to relieve skills training and meet new people. She now works there.

I had a lot of reservations about coming here. I was afraid when I contacted the centre of what people would think of me due to the way people perceive such centres that cater for women's needs. Members of my family wouldn't let me come here. I wasn't allowed here as there is a feeling that ideas would be put in to my head that would be deviant and wrong.

I first came to Roshni to meet other women and increase my social skills. I joined the English and computer classes as someone who came from Pakistan I couldn't speak English and was not encouraged to.

My husband wasn't happy with me coming here so I had to come here in secret, he now knows but that is due to changing attitudes. And over the years attitudes changed and now it's becoming slightly more acceptable for women to attend such places.

If it was not for such groups then I wouldn't know what my life would have been like; probably not speaking English and not knowing my rights and stuck at home cooking and cleaning. And that is not through the faults of my husband, because he is also subject to the same social norms as myself.

With me being here over the years has also changed my husband's attitudes and the family attitudes. Because he now knows there is a different way for things to happen he sees things differently, and would not suppress my views. It is better for us and our children.

You are raised a certain way and told to behave a certain way but that does not work here, and women need to know about places like this and more should be done to places like this because they are from the community and work with the community and they help a lot of women over the years who are forced into marriage or subjected to violence.

I now help the group as I am on the management committee, and help out in events such as the upcoming *Eid*.

Tanisha Jnagel, the community services team leader for Roshni Asian Women's Aid, a refuge in Nottingham, says:

❝ What you see is a change in the ideas that young people hold — but they still may not be able to exercise these choices ❞

– but at the same time I think that it is going down – even though it's still an unknown issue. You can only talk about what you see – not about what you don't see. Making people more aware of it makes them more willing to come and discuss it with you."

Others, however, warn that this growing willingness to discuss the issue is only slowly filtering down and changing the practices of more isolated communities. Tanisha Jnagel, the community services team leader for Roshni Asian Women's Aid, a refuge in Nottingham, says:

"What you see is a change in the ideas that young people hold – but they still may not be able to exercise these choices. What is changing is that in arranged marriages there is now much more a level of choice. Now you might be able to choose a partner more than before – but within a limited scale of class, background, religion, income – whereas before that wasn't the norm."

Almost all women's groups say that such changes will not, and cannot, happen 'overnight'. Most groups say that such changes in attitudes may take several generations to fully take effect.

Explaining changing attitudes

■ *Increased exposure to alternative cultures and lifestyles*

Many children of foreign origin brought up in the UK are becoming increasingly aware of other lifestyles which offer alternatives to belief system of their families and communities. While this is already occurring through exposure to other cultures through the media and the education system, tackling segregation can also raise awareness of women's rights.

Although many families of immigrant background attempt to prevent their children from being influenced by 'western' ideas and modes of behaviour, young people brought up in the UK are inevitably exposed to a range of concepts which challenge traditional ideas of acceptable behaviour. This process is occurring at schools, in the streets and in daily life, as well as through television, the media and popular culture. In many cases, this is leading younger generations to question imported ideas of honour. Humera Khan, co-founder of the An-Nisa Society, a women's advocacy group in Wembley, says:

> "Children up to adolescence, despite what the dynamics, are generally happy. Then suddenly when they reach adolescence they judge themselves on what they see in the mainstream culture through television or magazines; there is a feeling of dissatisfaction on the way they are living their life because the message from the media is strong."

Maureen Salmon, the interim-director of Forward, a group campaigning against FGM, says that many of these principles also apply to FGM. She says:

> "If you are in your country of origin, you see it [FGM] just as something that all the girls have done. And then suddenly you're in a society where it's not common and then for the first time you have to think about actually why you do it."

Ghazala Razzaq, co-ordinator for Roshni Asian Women's Re-

Ghazala Razzaq, co-ordinator for Roshni Asian Women's Resource Centre, a support group in Sheffield, says:

66 Times are now changing. The older women have accepted domestic violence. The younger women are willing to take a lot less in terms of abuse 99

source Centre, a support group in Sheffield, says:

> "Times are now changing. The older women have accepted domestic violence. The younger women are willing to take a lot less in terms of abuse. There is a lot more support here, and there are a lot more financially independent women in comparison with their parents' country."

This process might not necessarily apply to women brought to the UK from abroad to marry who might not speak English and may be uneducated and unaware of their legal rights. However, many believe that as women become more educated, financially independent and self-assertive, the pace of social change will accelerate. Ghayasuddin Siddiqui, the leader of the Muslim Parliament, says:

> "Now that women are starting to play an active role in all fields of life and becoming educated, their participation will become more critical to stopping this; they can play a leading role in saying that this is wrong. I don't think in fact that the campaign against these practices can succeed without women. But the problem is that once this is portrayed as a religious or cultural issue, it becomes a part of a person's identity."

Such growing pressure on traditional practices can force even conservative religious leaders to change their attitudes to issues such as honour and domestic violence. John Paton, who manages the Lancashire Family Mediation Service in Preston, was approached by a local imam who had found himself increasingly unable to offer helpful advice to young people. Paton says:

> "There are a lot of third generation Muslims who are no longer accepting the cultural norms of their parents. There are also issues around alcohol and drugs which families are aware of. They take these issues to the imam and he will try to resolve them. But he wasn't able to do so – they weren't listening to him, to put it bluntly."

Despite these signs, there is no guarantee that ideas of tolerance, non-violence and sexual equality will filter from mainstream society into all sectors of all immigrant communities. Indeed, growing ghetto-isation and the significant influence of conservative Muslim groups over government policy may significantly slow down this process against this to some degree. The consequences of such segregation are already visible in some segments of the orthodox Jewish community which have effectively isolated themselves from mainstream British society. Abigail Morris, the director of Jewish Women's Aid, a refuge in North London, says:

Ghayasuddin Siddiqui, the leader of the Muslim Parliament, says:

66 I don't think in fact that the campaign against these practices can succeed without women 99

123

ORTHODOX JEWISH MARRIAGES AND DIVORCES

According to orthodox Jewish law ("halacha" in Hebrew), marriage between a Jewish man and woman can only be entered into with full consent and by mutual agreement. In the UK a civil marriage takes place at the same time as the Jewish wedding – although some Ultra-Orthodox Jews may dispute the necessity of obtaining a civil marriage.

However problems may arise during divorce when civil and religious divorce proceedings take place independently. Ultra orthodox versions of Jewish law say that a marriage can only be ended by the husband, unless there are exceptional circumstances.

Divorce in Jewish law occurs when the husband gives a divorce decree, or "Get" in Hebrew, to his wife. This 'Get' is a special document drawn up by a Jewish court of law or "Beth Din". To be valid, the Get has to be accepted by the wife and this process must be witnessed by someone acting on behalf of the Beth Din court.

Should either marital partner refuse to play their part in the divorce ritual, the couple will remain married in the eyes of orthodox Jewish law, even if they have obtained a civil divorce. Should a couple fail to obtain a Jewish divorce, neither party can remarry through an orthodox Jewish ceremony.

Not being able to obtain an Orthodox Jewish divorce has different consequences for men and women. If the man has another child from another Jewish woman, the child will be regarded as legitimate under Jewish law – as long as, at the time of conception, its mother is unmarried and the legitimate child of a Jewish mother.

By contrast, if a Jewish woman who has not received a Get from her husband becomes pregnant by another man, the child will be seen as illegitimate under Jewish law. A child conceived in such circumstances will be accorded in Jewish law the status of being a "mamzer". Being a manzer – which can also refer to a child born from an incestuous union – has important social and religious penalties. For example, no mamzer may marry in a synagogue – except to another mamzer. Nor may any child of a mamzer.

One consequence of this arrangement is that men suffer only limited social penalties by not being divorced while women can be seriously disadvantaged and that, as a result, men have only limited incentive to grant their wives a divorce. As a result a Jewish woman whose husband is unwilling to grant her a Get is known in Hebrew as an "agunot", meaning a "chained woman".

In cases where a Jewish marriage has broken down, a man can use this situation in order to extract a more favourable divorce settlement – knowing that unless he grants his wife a get, she cannot have legitimate Jewish children. For example, a man can withhold the *Get* in order to obtain more money or property under a divorce settlement.

Since 2003 civil divorce courts in England have been granted extra powers intended to neutralise any potential bargaining advantage to be gained by either party refusing to grant or receive a *Get*.

Source: Getting your Get: Information for Jewish men and women in England about divorce according to Jewish law with articles, forms and explanations for lawyers. By Sharon Faith and Deanna Levine. http://www.gettingyourget.co.uk/.

"Women in the orthodox community tend to suffer more incidences of domestic violence before coming forward. We suspect there is a higher level [of domestic violence] in arranged marriages, some of the girls are very young, but we don't know exactly [the figures] because it is a very hard community to break into. But this is a guarded community and it is difficult area to get statistics on it."

Jews have lived in the UK for hundreds of years. The ability of some members of the orthodox community to remain isolated from so many trends affecting mainstream society illustrates the potential perils of the type of self-segregation sometimes favoured by more recent immigrants.

Role of NGOs

66 [Work] has to be done at primary school and infant school to tackle these attitudes as soon as possible. It needs to become part of the curriculum; it should be part of the citizenship agenda 99

Nazir Afzal, the Crown Prosecution Service lead on honour-based violence

NGOs and voluntary groups often conduct the majority of grassroots work with women at risk of violence. Often coming from the same background as the victims of honour-based violence, workers in such groups believe that their work in raising gender equality issues, holding workshops and working with schools can transform successfully challenge traditions of honour-based violence.

Many members of ethnic minority groups in the UK are suspicious of the government and the police. As a result, non-Governmental Organisations (NGOs) and voluntary organisations play a key role in challenging traditional ideas, promoting ideas of gender equality and condemning violence against women. Shaminder Ubhi, the director of Ashiana, a women's refuge in Leyton in East London, says:

> "What we find is perhaps interventions from people outside of the community are not that well received because sometimes it can be seen as intrusive; 'what the hell are you doing here' and 'what do you know about our community'. As a state or the police or government … there is a bit of a resistance … Similarly, I think it easier for us to go into the communities and speak to them as a local Asian women's group and talk about the issues and how they are affecting women and begin that dialogue and debate … My feeling and this organisation's feeling is that perhaps change must come from within."

In general, these groups aim to work with children, with victims of honour-based violence and with adult men and women who are at risk of such violence.

■ Working with children: challenging traditions

Almost all women's groups and those working in related areas believe that working extensively with schools is the best way to prevent ideas that honour-based violence is acceptable from being passed on to new generations.

Nazir Afzal, the Crown Prosecution Service lead on honour-based violence, says:

> "[Education to tackle causes of honour-based violence] has to be done at primary school and infant school to tackle these attitudes as soon as possible. It needs to become part of the curriculum; it should be part of the citizenship agenda. Some of the faith schools – particularly in East London have been quite good at this – it doesn't matter if a school is 90 per cent Asian – as long as they're getting the right sort of education."

In the absence of effective action by many branches of local government, several women's groups have begun independently working with nearby schools to make pupils and teachers more aware of the risks of forced marriage and honour-based violence. Such work generally aims to build young women's self-confidence in order to allow them to better resist family pressure and threats of violence, as well as seeking to raise awareness of the threats they can face. Ghazala Razzaq, co-ordinator of Roshni Asian Women's Resource Centre, a support group in Sheffield which works with schools, says:

> "We provide homework support and group work support in schools. We build their self-esteem and confidence, and we are looking at why

Abigail Morris, director of Jewish Woman's Aid, says:

66 I think unless you challenge young people on gender specifics in a fundamental way, then these abuses are going to be really difficult to eradicate in the future 99

these women at the age of 16 are dropping out and not achieving."

Jewish Woman's Aid has similarly found that outreach work at schools can be effective. The group estimates that its workers speak to several thousand children in Jewish schools every year. Abigail Morris, director of Jewish Woman's Aid, says:

> "I think unless you challenge young people on gender specifics in a fundamental way, then these abuses are going to be really difficult to eradicate in the future. I think the government could take the lead on this. I think it is important to look ahead and provide the education and the framework. I think Jewish women particularly feel more isolated, and with our school work we can eradicate this."

Other grassroots organisations use technology to reach those at risk of honour-based violence. For example, Birmingham Housing Association, through its project, Ashram, has produced short films aimed at raising awareness of honour-based violence and forced marriage within the Asian community. These films are shown to community leaders, support workers and others – sometimes at specially organised events in community centres. Muna Choudhury, Ashram's business development officer, says:

> "We distribute these films through the community and to the social workers to educate them and train them. Through the videos we provide training for front line staff for both the statutory and voluntary agencies. The DVDs also highlight mental health issues with Asian women so people are made aware. We believe this method is changing attitudes."

Nazir Afzal meanwhile cites the Miss Dorothy[115] organisation as an example of how women's groups can work with schools to raise awareness of issues through DVDs which discuss issues such as domestic violence and forced marriage, and providing information for teachers in easily accessible manner. Organisations campaigning against FGM have used similar tactics. Maureen Salmon, the interim-director of Forward, a London-based group which campaigns against the practice, says:

> "We've got six young people involved in our campaign – and they've done a DVD. Some of them – although more than 16 years old – weren't aware of the practice [FGM]. It's not something that's talked about in the home. They don't necessarily even talk about it with their mother even if she has had it done. But now these young people are standing up and saying something about this."

---

115 Further information is available at http://www.missdorothy.co.uk and www.missdorothy.com

Other examples of good practice come from abroad. Nazir Afzal, the lead on honour-based violence at the Crown Prosecution Service, highlights how the Swedish government has successfully raised awareness of honour-based violence among school children of Kurdish origin. He says:

> "The Swedes are very good at working with the Kurdish community. They have around 100,000 Kurds. They are particularly good at the prevention end of things; they are getting young people to go around schools saying what the options are for people who are under threat [of honour based violence]."

All women's groups say that due to lack of staff, funding and, on occasion, co-operation from schools, they cannot reach as many children as they need to. Most of their outreach work is usually aimed at telling children what to do if they face a forced marriage or honour-based domestic violence – rather than tackling the attitudes which cause honour-based crime.

■ Working with adults: changing attitudes

While many groups believe that it will be necessary to educate the very youngest generations in order to change future attitudes, others believe that it is still possible to change the attitudes of adults in order to help make honour-based violence socially and culturally unacceptable.

■ Working with women

Women's groups say that in order to tackle traditional ideas of honour, it is vital to work with women who have been victims of honour-based violence and with those who are at risk of such violence.

Rafaat Mughal, the director of the Joint Association of Nissa Trusts, a women's support group in North London, says that encouraging women to learn occupational skills and helping them build relationships with people from outside their family, can give them economic independence while also improving their overall confidence. She says:

> "We try and change the mindset by inviting them here to meet other people from the community who have achieved something and are respected. We expose them to other people and it proves successful. If I tell them then it's like I'm forcing them, but I bring experts in [to talk to them]."

Other women's groups say that even women who rarely leave

> 66 We changed our tack here and by doing that we have attracted more people by not imposing a set of values on anyone, as vulnerable women are then too afraid to come and men would be more hostile to us if they knew our intentions 99
>
> *Ghazala Razzaq, centre co-ordinator for Roshni Asian Women's Resource Centre, Sheffield*

their homes can be reached when they collect their children from school. Zahia Tatimahand, director of Kiran Asian Women's Aid, a refuge in Leytonstone in East London, says:

"We speak to them [mothers]; maybe do consultation at schools when they are picking up their kids. It needs to be done at their level and in a language they can understand by using simpler English or with interpreters."

Ghazala Razzaq, centre co-ordinator for Roshni Asian Women's Resource Centre, a support group in Sheffield, advocates using all possible channels to reach women at risk:

"We put leaflets in public places like schools and GPs' surgeries to advertise courses and group events. We also rely on word of mouth. For example many women have come to us with a friend. We also use our training courses [in English and sewing] to reach isolated women."

She also says that groups which present themselves as seeking to impose new ideologies on the community are often less successful than those which seek to work within existing community structures and which empower women through training and education rather than through overtly introducing new ideologies. She says:

"We changed our tack here and by doing that we have attracted more people by not imposing a set of values on anyone, as vulnerable women are then too afraid to come and men would be more hostile to us if they knew our intentions."

Others agree and say that communities which already feel under attack by politicians, the police and the media are unlikely to respond positively to further criticism of their culture. Humera Khan, co-founder of the An-Nisa Society, a women's advocacy group in Wembley, says:

Humera Khan, co-founder of the An-Nisa Society, a women's advocacy group in Wembley, says:

❝ If Muslims were less attacked [by the media] they would be more receptive to deal with their bad practices ❞

"If Muslims were less attacked [by the media] they would be more receptive to deal with their bad practices. Just like with FGM, they [the government] realised they had to find ways to understand that it is a norm with people and then deal with it. You got to make people feel less threatened if you are asking them to change a deep-rooted cultural practice."

But while groups working in communities which are receptive to new ideas are able to use sewing classes and other forms of training to reach potentially vulnerable women, in other communities women who contact any type of women's group can be seen as bringing shame on their family and the community. However, as long as a few women are willing and able to break traditions, this encourages others to similarly challenge traditional cultural practices thus slowly pushing the community as a whole towards redefining its notions of honour and a woman's acceptable behaviour. One South Asian woman, who requested anonymity, who has used services provided by Roshni Asian Women's Resource Centre in Sheffield for over ten years, describes how this change can occur. She says:

> "At first I had a lot of reservations about coming here. I was afraid when I contacted the centre of what people would think of me. Members of my family wouldn't let me come here. I wasn't allowed [to come] here as there is a feeling that ideas would be put in to my head. I first came to Roshni to meet other women and looked to increase my social skills and went on the English and computer classes. My husband wasn't happy with me coming here but it has now become more acceptable for people to come to Roshni."

The woman is now an active member of the group who encourages other women to join the group's courses. Women who have been through such courses or who have survived domestic violence can play an important role in changing attitudes. Other women's groups stress the importance of providing communities with positive role models. Rafaat Mughal, the director of the Joint Association of Nissa Trusts in North London, says:

> "We bring them role models for talks. Sometimes it's women who have been here and have been successful. The majority here are Muslims, but we are a mixed group and we encourage them to integrate."

In many cases such role models can be controversial, however, and may risk putting communities further on the defensive. Maureen Salmon , the interim-director of Forward, points to the example of prominent secularist and atheist Ayaan Hirsi Ali, the Somali-born former Dutch MP who campaigns against FGM. Salmon says:

> "We're living in a celebrity culture … Generally, in terms of the Somali community, they don't see her [Ayaan] as the right sort of role model … I personally think it does help but others say that this isn't the sort of role model that we should listen to."

Women's groups who use a variety of role models are likely to enjoy the greatest success in tackling honour-based domestic violence.

Maureen Salmon, the interim-director of Forward, says:

66 We're living in a celebrity culture … Generally, in terms of the Somali community, they don't see her [Ayaan] as the right sort of role model … I personally think it does help but others say that this isn't the sort of role model that we should listen to 99

Mohamed Baleela, team leader at the Domestic Violence Intervention Project in Hammersmith in West London, says

66 We cannot defeat violence in the community without having the community on our side 99

■ *Working with men*

Many workers in women's groups also emphasise the importance of working with men as a way to achieve deep rooted cultural and social changes.

Batool Al-Toma, the head of the National Muslim Women's Advisory Group and an advisor on women's affairs for the Mosque and Imams National Advisory Board (MINAB), says:

❝ Texts from the Quran can be used as a deterrent to domestic violence ❞

Rania Hafez, principle lecturer in education at the University of East London, says:

> "The role of male members in the community speaking out against honour-based crimes is crucial. There should be greater work done with men in terms of them understanding equity and equality."

Mohamed Baleela, team leader at the Domestic Violence Intervention Project in Hammersmith in West London, runs a violence prevention programme through working with male perpetrators of domestic violence. He also works with Islamic organisations in West London, such as the Muslim Cultural Heritage Centre, in an attempt to raise awareness of domestic violence. He says:

> "We have a violence prevention programme, which tries to help male perpetrators of domestic violence. If their English is not good enough I can hold one-to-one sessions with them [in Arabic]. Our outreach work consists of raising awareness of domestic violence within the wider community. We also work very closely with imams and community leaders on this issue. We cannot defeat violence in the community without having the community on our side."

One man who has been through the programme says:

> "I have spent a year living away from my children and wife. I have greatly missed them and it is a great joy to be with them again. Programmes like the one I attended have helped in my understanding the issues and allows me to control and channel my anger into constructive things."

Mohammad Beleela estimates 25 per cent of the men who go through his programme stop abusing their wives and 50 per cent stop using violence but continue to use psychological and emotional pressure to control them. The remaining 25 per cent, he says, do not stop using physical violence against their wives.

Role of progressive religious groups

There are many examples of how religious scriptures can be used to challenge the attitudes held by perpetrators of violence towards women. Some of the most positive examples of this process come from the Muslim community.

131

Many people who work in the women's groups and in the voluntary sector believe that modern interpretations of religious scriptures can be used to tackle violence against women. Batool Al-Toma, the head of the National Muslim Women's Advisory Group and an advisor on women's affairs for the Mosque and Imams National Advisory Board (MINAB), says:

"Texts from the Quran can be used as a deterrent to domestic violence."

Hassan Safour, a project officer dealing with refugee and integration issues at the Muslim Welfare House at Finsbury Park, says quotations from the Quran and Hadith (collections of the sayings of Muhammad) can be used to tell people that violence against women is un-Islamic. He runs awareness session with community leaders and social workers to help them understand the extent of the problem and to identify and tackle potential incidents of violence. He says:

"Better training of community leaders should include the training of imams – informing them of the social and psychological consequences of domestic violence. Every day imams get women coming up to them with questions about these things. The women are already in the right place and we could offer guidance and help."

One imam who has acted to tackle honour-based violence is Ibrahim Mogra who is the chair of the Muslim Council of Britain's Inter Faith Relations committee as well as being an imam in Leicester, says:

"Personally [I think] it is not possible for men to use Islam for violence against women because there are no teachings in Islam that allow such acts. However, if the imam is hell bent on promoting this stuff, they can misinterpret, and twist and bring in more cultural dimension than a religious one. The Messenger [Muhammad] said 'the best of you are those who treat women in the best way'. On his death bed he said 'I advise you to treat women kindly'. I don't how with all these teachings, people can teach violence, maybe it is a personal problem for them and they have not understood the true meaning of Islam."

Other Muslim groups have also used religious texts to tackle violence against women. In Accrington, for example, the Lancashire Council of Mosques holds regular events for women in the community[116] and one of the town's mosques regularly hosts meetings for various voluntary groups to discuss ways to tackle hon-

66 **Personally it is not possible for them to use Islam for violence against women because there are no teachings in Islam that allow such acts, however if the imam is hell bent on promoting this stuff, they can misinterpret, and twist and bring in a more cultural dimension than a religious one** 99

Ibrahim Mogra, the chair of the Masjid and Community Affairs Committee of the MCB

---

116 The Lancashire Council of Mosques, based in Blackburn, is an umbrella group that says it represents "all mosques and religious teaching institutions in Lancashire". http://www.lancashiremosques.com/

our-based violence. John Paton, the manager of the Lancashire Family Mediation Service in Preston which works with imams in Accrington to promote awareness of women's rights, says:

> "The role of the mosque – to my mind – is very positive … We had two to three meetings in the big mosque in Accrington in which we gave presentations and talked about what we wanted to do. There was also real engagement from quite a large number of community organisations – also involvement from the police who were very positive."

The Muslim Parliament, mainly through the work of Ghayasuddin Siddiqui, its leader, has also tackled FGM, forced marriage and honour-based domestic violence. In association with the Muslim Women's Institute the group has launched a "Stop Forced Marriages Campaign"[117] with the aim of creating awareness within Muslim communities. Prior to this, the Muslim Parliament produced practical guides for those intending to have a Muslim marriage in Britain.[118] Siddiqui, believes that, as a result of these and other measures, such subjects are increasingly debated openly in the Muslim community. He says:

> "Even child abuse is becoming a topic possible to discuss. For example, some people who have made a new magazine called Suburb Magazine [119] in Bradford recently contacted me and asked me to write an article about child abuse. They saw my website and saw that I was the only person talking about these things. A lot of people are finding out these things through the internet – it's become very easy now."

Although many – and perhaps most – mosques still shun campaigns against domestic violence, more Muslim religious leaders than ever before are now working with women's groups in the UK. Mohamed Baleela, team leader at the Domestic Violence Intervention Plan in Hammersmith in West London, says:

> "We try to be the link between mosques, community centres and Islamic centres and outside agencies. Regents Park Mosque, Muslim Heritage Centre, Westbourne Park and Al Muntada al-Islami are all mosques we work with. We work also with other smaller mosques. These Islamic centres have a lot of facilities we can use, and the majority of Arab Muslims go there."

---

117 *Forced Marriage*, a briefing paper by the Muslim Parliament of Great Britain is available online at http://www.muslimparliament.org.uk/marriage.htm A study of Forced Marriages produced by the Muslim Women's Institute in association with the Muslim Parliament Thinking About Marriage by Ruqaiyyah Waris Maqsood (London, 2005) is available online at http://www.muslimparliament.org.uk/Documentation/ThinkingaboutMarriage.pdf

118 The Muslim Parliament's *Getting Married – Some Guidelines* is available online at http://www.muslimparliament.org.uk/marriage_guidelines.htm.

119 *Suburb Magazine* is not available online.

Similar positive developments are occurring in London's Sikh communities. Some Sikh temples in West London have begun putting up posters against domestic violence for example. Ila Patel, director of the Asha Project in Streatham, says:

> "It is a sign that some communities are finally acknowledging it. It is also significant that women with no recourse to public funds are being housed in temples and mosques."

The progress that many religious leaders have made towards making honour-related violence socially unacceptable in their communities illustrates how religious leaders can play a highly positive role in ending violence against women.

Government successes

Many voluntary groups say that the British government – particularly the Foreign and Commonwealth Office (FCO) and the police service – is beginning to understand the issue of honour-based violence and take steps to address the problem.

Although most women's groups say that the government is not yet doing enough to tackle honour-based violence, many also say that the government has begun to take steps to tackle the problem. Shahien Taj, director of the Henna Foundation, a women's group in Cardiff, says:

> "We have been working with South Cardiff police for nine years, and they have started to understand these issues [honour crimes]. Now the police have realised that they have to work with us; ringing us and asking us to meet with their clients because they are realising that they need our help because sometimes they make things worse."

In particular, the government has worked through the FCO and the police, backed by legislation where appropriate, to deter and punish perpetrators and open avenues of escape for victims and potential victims of violence. Many of those interviewed for this study say that if the government further prioritised the tackling of honour-based violence, created a co-ordinated national strategy and allocated more resources to the issue, the rate of honour-related abuse and violence would soon begin to decline.

■ *Growing police awareness*

In recent years, the police have dramatically stepped up their attempts to tackle instances of honour-based violence. This has

66 The Forced Marriage Unit . . . is excellent. They are proactive, they take active steps, follow up and help girls; that unit is good 99

Anne-Marie Hutchinson, a lawyer specialising in honour-related crimes for Dawson Coronwell in London

happened partly as a result of increased pressure from the public, the media and politicians but also through the commitment of numerous individual police officers.

Philip Balmforth, vulnerable persons' officer (Asian women), says:

❝ A person in my position could reach vulnerable people much quicker than a volunteer group because I am hiding behind a badge that says 'West Yorkshire Police' and because I am seen as someone in authority. If I was seen as a worker from the voluntary group then people would not have that kind of conversation with me and I would not be able to help as many people as possible ❞

The police have been particularly spurred into action by the high-profile murders of Rukhsana Naz and Heshu Yones. More recently, the police have had to reassess their approach again following the murder of Banaz Mahmod, a Kurdish woman who had unsuccessfully appealed for the police to protect her against her family. The police's growing awareness of honour-based violence is leading them to adopt new approaches. Recently, for example, police have also begun using more sophisticated techniques to pursue perpetrators of honour-based violence. Nazir Afzal, the Crown Prosecution Service lead on honour-based violence, says:

"We are now using techniques usually used to fight organised crime to tackle this – we're using covert officers, listening devices and other methods. It's all perfectly legal but we are finding that the only way to tackle this is to use techniques that are unusual for family cases. That's because we don't see this as domestic violence – it's beyond that. The murder of Banaz was so brutal that it was a clear warning to others; it was a way of saying 'don't step out of line or this could be you' ... We've started to realise how organised this is – and that this is what distinguishes it from ordinary domestic violence when you just have one-on-one violence; a husband beating his wife for instance. In the last few years I've not dealt with a single case of honour-based violence that didn't involve multiple perpetrators."

Almost all women's refuges can narrate stories of individual police officers who have gone to great lengths to protect women who are at risk and to gain prosecutions against perpetrators. Ila Patel, the director of the Asha Project in Streatham, says:

"We had a case when the police actually went to the Punjab region in India because someone had been killed there and that person had been at the refuge. The police started an investigation after examining an insurance claim [her husband] had made."

In some cases, individual police forces have implemented their own one-off strategies against honour-based violence. In Bradford, for example, Philip Balmforth (a former police inspector who had worked on honour-related issues since 1988) was appointed as the district's vulnerable person's officer (Asian Women). Balmforth says that this job put him in a unique position to help women at risk of violence:

"A person in my position could reach vulnerable people much quicker than a volunteer group because I am hiding behind a badge that says

'West Yorkshire Police' and because I am seen as someone in authority. If I was seen as a worker from the voluntary group then people would not have that kind of conversation with me and I would not be able to help as many people as possible."

Balmforth says his unusual position – combined with the fact that there is as yet no specific criminal law against forced marriage – means that women feel free to consult with him; they are reassured that he is in a position of authority and can help them while also knowing that their family will not be prosecuted without their consent. He says:

"99.9 per cent of all my clients – and I have 4,000 on my books – always say: 'You are from the police, are you going to get people in trouble? Because if you are, we are not going to talk to you' … We have always been proactive in West Yorkshire with race issues, to try and solve the problem before it becomes a problem."

In Accrington, Lancashire, the police service has been similarly responsive and has recently begun a ground-breaking initiative to bring together community organisations, imams, mosques and domestic violence organisations in order to jointly tackle honour-based violence. Those involved in the scheme say that the police's enthusiastic involvement played a key part in giving an official stamp of authority to the project. John Paton, the manager of Lancashire Family Mediation Service in Preston, says:

"There was also real engagement from quite a large number of community organisations – also involvement from the police who were very positive. By the end of this process, when there was no doubt that violence was occurring, we were able to sell them this project. "

The Home Office has also launched a new trial system called 'Third Party Reporting' which allows victims of Domestic Violence to report incidents to community organisations rather than directly to the police. This system – initially intended to encourage ethnic minorities to report racism – has reportedly helped women who did not trust the police or who were afraid to be seen going into a police station. Hassan Safour, the project officer in refugee and integration issues at the Muslim Welfare House in Finsbury Park, says:

"'Third Party Reporting' gives women the opportunity to report domestic abuse to a social worker who is trained – which means you can report a crime to someone other than the police. We've received training so we can do all the paperwork which means we can do a case in about two hours. However it takes 72 hours to process so in an emergency we tell people to go to the police. With the 'Third Party Reporting', people can speak Arabic to us and they're more comfortable than going to the police. We also provide language support for them."

Despite these localised successes, police initiatives at a national level are often hampered by a lack of co-operation from other government departments. Yasmin Rehman, who wrote the draft ACPO (Association of Chief Police Officers) strategy on honour-based violence, says that none of the social services departments approached to give feedback on the draft responded. She says:

> "We haven't had any responses from social services departments which I think is deeply sad."

Such anecdotal evidence suggests that lack of communication between different branches of government is substantially affecting the government's ability to tackle honour-based violence.

■ *Foreign and Commonwealth Office*

The Foreign and Commonwealth Office (FCO) has instituted a number of procedures to help women who are being forced into a marriage or who are at risk of honour killings. Most significantly, the FCO has established a Forced Marriage Unit (FMU) which aims to intervene to stop forced marriages happening. Every year the FMU deals with between 250-300 cases of forced marriage.[120]

The service also runs a helpline which offers advice to victims and professionals and holds around 70 outreach meetings every year. The FCO also produces a number of print and electronic guides for police officers, social workers, education and health professionals. The guides are uniformly well-thought out and clearly presented. Among the FMU's most notable successes was to rescue an 11-year old British-Bengali girl from marriage in May 2007.[121]

Anne Marie Hutchinson, a lawyer who specialises in honour-related crime and who has advised the FCO on the issue, says of the FMU:

> "They are excellent. They are proactive, they take active steps, follow up and help girls; that unit is good."

Many women who have used the FCO's services praise its profes-

---

120 Forced Marriage (CivilProtection) Bill: Research paper. 28 June 2007 http://www. parliament.uk/commons/lib/research/rp2007/rp07-056.pdf

121 *BBC*: 'Girl, 11, rescued from marriage' 8 May 2007 [http://news.bbc.co.uk/1/hi/uk/6635191.stm]

sionalism and attention to detail. 'Saamiya', a 16-year old who was taken to Pakistan for a forced marriage in summer 2007, was rescued by the FMU after someone with details of her cases alerted Crime Stoppers Anonymous. Within days, FCO officials had travelled to her family's village in rural Pakistan and intervened to halt the marriage. The girl says:

> "The Foreign Office actually came and asked me if I wanted to go back. My dad was there so I said 'no' and that I was happy here. But they asked my dad to leave the room and then they asked me again and I said yes, that I wanted to go home. When I arrived at the airport in England, I had two armed coppers on each side of me and the social services were there as well."

'Saamiya' is now staying in a women's refuge in northern England and hopes to resume her full-time education. Despite these successes,, the FCO's methods are not aimed at tackling the cultural roots of forced marriages. Instead, they largely aim at helping women escape from forced marriages and from similar situations where they might be subject to violence. In addition, the FMU's small staff means that its ability to deal with even existing cases is limited. Perhaps as a result of this understaffing and inadequate funding, the FMU is often unable to perform the necessary level of outreach and raising awareness work. 'Saamiya' says:

> "I knew it [the FMU] existed but I didn't know how to get hold of them. And when I went to Pakistan I just thought that it was a holiday."

Others also say that the FCO should do more grassroots work to reach those potentially at risk of a forced marriage and other abuses. Kubir Randhawala, director of Asian Family Counselling Service in Southall in West London, says:

> "The Community Liaison Office [of the FCO] has done a great job in raising awareness and providing training. They have highlighted much more, but there needs to be smaller groups working within the community."

The FCO can also be slow at identifying emerging problems. In particular, it has not yet fully responded to changes in the ethnic balance of immigrants in the UK and the FMU has so far largely concentrated on forced marriages occurring among families from Pakistan, India and Bangladesh. It may be many years before it begins to recognise and tackle similar problems in the Middle East and East Africa.

■ *Legislation*

The government has sought to tackle honour-based violence through by instituting new laws. In particular, two laws against forced marriage and FGM have sought to criminalise specific forms of honour-based violence.

The Forced Marriage (Civil Protection) Act received Royal Ascent on 27 July 2007 and, when it comes into force in late 2008, will allow victims of forced marriage to pursue perpetrators through civil courts but does not necessarily force the police to act in suspected cases of forced marriage.[122] Parliament took a different approach towards tackling FGM. The Female Genital Mutilation Act[123] of 2003 criminalised not only perpetrators of the act but also made it a crime to help anyone else – in the UK or overseas – perform the operation.

Although no-one has yet been convicted under the FGM law, women's groups say that its high-profile launch – in regional, national and ethnic media – has probably deterred people from carrying out the operation on their daughters, whether in the UK or abroad. Maureen Salmon, the interim-director of Forward, which campaigns against FGM, says:

> "The police campaign on this has been one of the most successful which they've ever done on the issue – people taking their children outside the UK to have this done will be aware that this is illegal …
> If you talk to Somali community leaders they say that they feel their community is being looked at."

But while the explicit criminalisation of FGM sent out a clear message to communities that their traditional, practice was considered illegal by the British government, the Forced Marriage Bill was issued with little fanfare. This may have been an attempt by the government to please advocates of the bill without antagonising pressure groups like the Muslim Council of Britain which had campaigned against it. One individual who was involved in drafting the bill says:

> "The civil marriage bill will help. The consultation was a real consultation and it was split 50:50 between people who wanted it to be made a criminal offence and those who didn't. It was argued that making it

---

122 The text of the Forced Marriage (Civil Protection) Act 2007 can be found online at http://www.opsi.gov.uk/acts/acts2007/pdf/ukpga_20070020_en.pdf] The act is due to come into force in autumn 2008, according to a press release issued by the Ministry of Justice from 28 November 2007 [http://www.justice.gov.uk/news/newsrelease281107a.htm].

123 The text of the Female Genital Mutilation Act 2003 can be found at http://www.opsi. gov.uk/ACTS/acts2003/pdf/ukpga_20030031_en.pdf

a criminal offence would deter people from coming forward because they wouldn't want to get their families in trouble. The government has agreed to hold a review in several years time to see if it is working and then, if necessary, to reconsider going down the route of criminalisation. I think this is basically the right approach – although I had my doubts at the time."

Voluntary organisations working in these areas warn that without prosecutions under either law, however, the government may lose interest in pursuing potential perpetrators. Maureen Salmon, the interim-director of Forward, says:

"From the point of view of the police it is important to get a prosecution so that this can be kept on their agenda. If the police don't get a prosecution the government will turn around and say that maybe this practice isn't happening after all. The police are aware that this is happening but so far they can't get the quality of information from communities to really tackle this issue."

It remains to be seen how effective these two pieces of legislation will be in preventing honour-based violence.

CHAPTER 8:

Recommendations: how the government can accelerate change

So far, the British government has been reluctant to take the measures needed to stop honour-based violence. This policy, or lack of, has caused considerable human suffering while also ensuring that the burden of tackling these practices and traditions has fallen on charities and unpaid volunteers who are often themselves the survivors of honour-based of violence. Shahien Taj, director of the Henna Foundation, a woman's group in Cardiff, says:

TACKLING HONOUR-CRIMES: HOW INDIA TACKLED SATI (THE RITUAL BURNING OF WIDOWS)

In India, the once-commonplace Hindu practice of Sati (the ritual burning of widows) has been virtually stamped out through laws, policing, theological reform and changing attitudes.

In 1987, the government passed the Commission of Sati (Prevention) Act which outlawed all glorification and advocacy of the practice.Mark In addition the law reversed the burden of proof, requiring defendants to prove they had not abetted Sati and also allowed for anyone who inherited property as the result of sati to be barred from receiving that inheritance. The law slowed incidents of Sati to a trickle. [The text of the Act is online at the website of India's Ministry of Women and Child Development. http://wcd.nic.in/commissionofsatiprevention.htm]

In 2007 the government outlined plans to finally eliminate the practice. The government now plans to amend the 1987 act to allow prosecutions against all witnesses to the act of Sati and against whole villages and communities if necessary. The amendments would also raise the minimum prison sentences. Village councils could also be tried if they failed to report a Sati case. "Even though we have just a few recorded cases of sati annually, even one is too many," an official from the women and child development ministry said Mark.

[Reuters: India to toughen law on custom of burning widows. 17 July 2007. http://www.reuters.com/article/latestCrisis/idUS-DEL55004]

"The voluntary sector is sometimes treated as a statutory organisation by the government and too much work is carried out by us."

Police working in the field, women's refuge workers and the victims of honour-based violence are almost unanimous in saying that tougher measures are needed to tackle the root causes of such crimes. Sana Bukhari, a support worker for Ashiana, a refuge in Sheffield, says:

"The government should tighten its immigration laws and the girls here should be encouraged to work. The government should investigate things properly. There is a lot of pressure on the voluntary sector and the government could take some of that pressure off."

The government also needs to stop taking advice on the issue from self-appointed 'community leaders', such as the Muslim Council of Britain (MCB), who are doing little or nothing on the ground to tackle honour-based violence. Mohamed Baleela, a team leader at the Domestic Violence Intervention Project in Hammersmith in West London, says:

"A lot of imams will go to the government and media, giving a very positive view of the community and of Sharia law, but it is not always strictly true. We need someone to put pressure on them. Sometimes I see people on television and on the radio and they say how Sharia law does this and that. But I listen to it and think 'do we live on the same planet?' I am a practicing Muslim but we have to say there is a problem. The best way to tackle issues is to tackle them head on."

As part of this, the government needs to stop seeing women of immigrant backgrounds as people who are not expected to have the same rights, hopes and values as native British women. Shaminder Ubhi, the director of Ashiana, a women's refuge in Leyton in East London, says:

"They [the Government] need to integrate honour crimes, and forced marriages into the general domestic violence framework. We need to look at it as an overall violence against women. [But] we [also] need to realise that different communities need different responses."

Taking real action against the root causes of honour-based violence will not only help end human rights abuses committed against women but will also have a range of positive consequences for immigrant communities and wider society. Nazir Afzal, the Crown Prosecution Service lead on honour-based violence, says:

"You can solve a lot of problems by tackling honour-based violence. By tackling this you can improve women's rights, improve woman's edu-

Shaminder Ubhi, the director of Ashiana, a women's refuge in Leyton in East London, says:

66 They [the Government] need to integrate honour crimes, and forced marriages into the general domestic violence framework. We need to look at it as an overall violence against women. [But] we [also] need to realise that different communities need different responses 99

Mohamed Baleela, a team leader at the Domestic Violence Intervention Project in Hammersmith in West London, says:

66 I am a practicing Muslim but we have to say there is a problem. The best way to tackle issues is to tackle them head on 99

cation, improve community cohesion and tackle segregation. You're also in a position to increase the wealth of communities because you can get women into the job market. In effect you're also attacking radicalisation by a different route. This is also a means to build closer links with international bodies and other countries since this is such a transnational problem. You might think that tackling this issue is just about solving the position of women in certain communities but in fact it's a way to tackle real societal issues and to create a lot of goodwill on all sides."

The government should also examine how other countries have sought to tackle honour-violence. In India, centuries of reform have succeeded in virtual stamping out the Hindu practice of Sati, or widow burning [See factbox]. Turkey has taken a similar approach to tackling honour killings, changing the law to allow prosecution of anyone who helps plan honour killings.[124]

In parts of Europe, a range of similar strategies have been employed in an effort to end violence against women. In Spain, in 2004, Mohamed Kamal Mustafa, a Muslim imam was given an 18-month suspended prison sentence for "inciting violence against women" in his book Women in Islam.[125] The book was also withdrawn from Islamic centres in Spain after a lawsuit was filed by 90 women's groups. In France, Yusuf al-Qaradawi's book The Lawful and the Prohibited in Islam was similarly prohibited – albeit briefly – for also condoning wife-beating.[126] In Denmark in 2006, nine members of a single family were convicted for taking part in, and assisting, in the honour killing of Ghazala Khan, an 18 year-old woman of Pakistan origin.[127]

Recommendations

It is self-evident that the government should take all necessary steps to tackle honour-based violence. Yet at the same time there are real concerns that an overly aggressive approach could make minority communities – and particularly Muslim ones – more suspicious of the police and the government, and indeed, entrench some people's determination to defend traditional ideas

---

124 *The Economist* 'A dishonourable practice' Apr 12th 2007 http://www.economist.com/world/europe/displaystory.cfm?story_id=9009023

125 *BBC*: 'Imam rapped for wife-beating book'. 14 January 2004. http://news.bbc.co.uk/1/hi/world/europe/3396597.stm

126 *The Guardian*: 'Cleric hits back at uniformed critics' by Faisal al-Yufai. 12 July 2004. http://www.guardian.co.uk/uk_news/story/0,3604,1258933,00.html

127 *BBC*: 'Jail for Denmark 'honour' killing'. 29 June 2006. http://news.bbc.co.uk/1/hi/world/europe/5128206.stm

and attitudes from outside interference and influence. Any action taken to prevent honour-crimes should therefore balance its potential success against any potential damage that such policies will cause to wider community cohesion.

■ *Low impact:*

❖ Improve police knowledge
Police need to be more aware of the nature of honour-based violence. A pool of officers specialising in tackling honour-based violence should be established in each district.

❖ Reform the 'No Recourse to Public Funds' rule
Women suffering from domestic violence should be made exempt from the 'No Recourse' rule on condition that they undertake language and career training. This will enable women to flee abusive situations and also help them become financially independent in the long-term. [Fines should also be introduced for those who 'abandon spouses']

❖ Greater support for women's groups
Local and central government should extend greater support to women's groups. This can include greater financial support and greater access to schools and local authority premises.

❖ Consult wider range of women's groups
The government relies excessively on the Southall Black Sisters for information and advice. The government should instead consult with a broader range of women's groups from around the UK which actually carry out on-on-the-ground work with victims of honour-based violence.

❖ Unified government strategy
A single strategy to tackle honour-based violence is needed to co-ordinate action by the police, the health services, local authorities, the social services and central government. Government agencies also need to agree on a definition of honour-based violence.

❖ Foreign policy
Foreign policy should aim to encourage other countries – and especially Pakistan, Bangladesh and Kurdistan – to improve women's rights. This will help to change attitudes among immigrants from these regions who live in the UK.

❖ Extradition treaties with Pakistan and Iraqi Kurdistan
Many women have been murdered by men who then fled to Pakistan and Kurdistan. At present there is no formal system to have them extradited to the UK.

■ *Medium impact:*

❖ **Improve information flow to women at risk**

Information on women's legal rights in the UK and the support available to victims of domestic violence should be made available to all brides arriving in the UK on marriage visas. This could be done at airports by women fluent in the appropriate languages.

❖ **Criminalise forced marriages**

Making forced marriages a civil offence has not worked. A high profile law to criminalise forced marriage is needed to tell communities that this practice is wrong and that people who carried out forced marriages will be held accountable.

❖ **Punish accomplices in honour killings and domestic violence**

People who seek to impede police investigations or withhold evidence should be held accountable. Those who help track down women who are then subjected to violence should also be prosecuted.

❖ **Tackle breaches of confidentiality**

Existing rules which prohibit local government employees from leaking National Insurance details or tax records to women's families should be enforced and strengthened if necessary. This should also apply to policemen and councillors who give out confidential information.

❖ **Tackle ideas of honour schools**

Schools should play a key role in ending honour-based violence. Children must be taught sexual equality and that violence against women is wrong. Schools can work with immigrant-focused refuges and women's groups to raise awareness of issues and of the assistance available to those at risk.

■ *High impact:*

❖ **Accelerate integration**

More training and educational opportunities should be offered to women from minority communities to enable them to enter the job market. Government-produced leaflets in foreign languages should be reduced to encourage greater fluency in English.

❖ **Punish those who advocate domestic violence or honour killings**

People who incite or encourage violence against women in print, media or at public meetings should be prosecuted. Similar laws which criminalise incitement to other forms of violence already exist.

145

❖ **Educate men of the costs of honour-based violence**
Government agencies, the media and NGOs should do more to tell
men from South Asian and Middle Eastern backgrounds why honour-based violence against women is wrong. Often men are not fully
aware of the cost of practices like FGM and forced marriages which
are carried out by female family members.

❖ **Find new community and religious leaders**
The government should not deal with religious individuals and groups
or 'community leaders' unless they have a demonstrable track record
of acting to prevent violence against women.

❖ **Tackle chain migration**
Raise the minimum age for those entering the UK on a marriage visa
from abroad from 18 to 21. Also make fluency in English and educational qualifications an additional entry requirement. This will accelerate integration and also tackle specific issues like forced marriage.

In many cases, it could be necessary to tailor such strategies to
take account of regional, ethnic and cultural variations within
the UK.

CHAPTER 9

Conclusion

Violence against women occurs in all societies and cultures and in all parts of the world. In the UK, such violence has been tackled over the last few decades through new laws, awareness-raising campaigns and a zero-tolerance approach tailored to changing specific aspects of mainstream British culture. This policy has largely succeeded in reducing domestic violence and making such violence socially unacceptable. As a result, domestic violence is today widely seen as morally wrong and as a criminal act.[128]

A similar approach is now needed to bring about a comparable change among some of the UK's immigrant groups. At present, ideas of honour which fuel violence against women are common in sectors of British society which originate in the Middle East and South Asia. In some cases, particularly among Pakistani communities in the North of England, such attitudes appear to be becoming more entrenched in people's cultures and identities through increasing segregation, rising religious radicalism and the development of a 'them-and-us' attitude to mainstream society. Frequently, ideas of sexual honour are perpetuated as a counterpoint to a mainstream British culture which community and religious leaders frequently dismiss as corrupt, worthless and immoral. In many cases, these factors are combining to make ideas of honour the core of many immigrants' identities.

So far, government attempts to tackle honour-based crimes have been inconclusive. Laws have been passed to criminalise specific acts of violence (such as Female Genital Mutilation) while police officers and the voluntary sector have aimed to protect women at acute risk of immediate violence. These attempts have avoided tackling the roots of the violence. The government appears to have hoped that honour-based violence would simply fade away as immigrants integrated into mainstream society. This approach has not worked and in many cases social services have failed to protect women from violence.

If the government wishes to end honour-based violence against women it must change the aspects of immigrants' cultures which

---

128 For example a July 2005 report by the Home Office found that between 1995 and 2004/5 reported incidents of domestic violence fell by 59%. It seems likely that this change is real rather than reflective of changes in how such crimes are recorded. *Crime in England and Wales 2004/2005* Sian Nicholas, David Povey, Alison Walker and Chris Kershaw (Home Office Statistical Bulletin, July 2005) [http://www.homeoffice.gov.uk/rds/pdfs05/hosb1105.pdf p.19]

lead directly to violence against women. Such violence against women was once accepted in mainstream British society; today such violence is taboo and forbidden. South Asian and Middle Eastern communities now must similarly redefine honour. At present many of these communities see the ability to control women as an indicator of male power and status. They instead need to redefine a strong man as one who is not afraid to let his daughters lead their own lives; a man whose image and reputation is too great to be troubled by rumours concerning his female relatives' sexual behaviour. Only when such core attitudes are changed, will honour-based violence against women end.

And yet, despite the government's non-interventionist approach, changes are happening. Many men and women from South Asia and the Middle East – both newly arrived and those raised in the UK – are moving to challenge traditional gender roles and question the authority of religious leaders, tribal authority figures and family elders. This has been most obvious in outward-looking Hindu communities which embrace the UK's educational and economic opportunities and who are open to new ideas and cultural practices. The moral disapproval expressed by the UK's majority towards minority practices such as forced marriages, honour killings and female genital mutilation is also having an effect. Practices carried out openly in people's countries of origin have now been driven underground. Traditions which were once seen as honourable are now increasingly seen as embarrassing or shameful; as things that should be hidden and denied. Immigrant communities – and even the most reactionary religious leaders – are showing themselves not to be immune to the moral disapproval of the wider public – and willing to change and reform as a result.

The ultimate spread of such attitudes is by no means certain however. Many women activists who have publicly challenged these practices have received death threats and now live and work with police alarms in their homes and offices. Some have been forced to flee their home towns altogether, to live in secret and in a state of perpetual fear. Men who have stood up in religious institutions and community centres to denounce violence against women have been beaten up. Time and time again, conservative religious leaders have sought to portray women's activists as improper and shameful and have sought to systematically block their activities. At least one woman activist, Caneze Riaz in Accrington, has been murdered for publicly questioning community attitudes and defending women's rights.

The defence of traditional practices by individuals and communities has implications not only for women but for society as a whole. Women's groups have reported that many senior Asian policemen and councillors openly put their loyalty to their culture, community and religion before their loyalty to the rule of law. Informal nationwide networks of taxi drivers, community elders and religious groups now exist to co-operate to track down and punish, with death if necessary, those who break community traditions and offend their religious codes. High profile Islamic organisations have repeatedly tried to block attempts by the government, the police and the judiciary to tackle the violent abuse of women by arguing that the community will feel 'victimised' by any laws aimed to halt the violence. Elected officials – of all ethnicities – have sought to block the activities of women's groups for fear of offending Asian voters. Most troubling of all, perhaps, is the increasingly widespread belief that where religious and cultural practices conflict with British laws, traditions should take priority. Unless the government takes action soon, these practices and attitudes will become more commonplace.

Women's groups also say that the branches of government – the legislature, the police, schools, elected officials and local authorities – are not taking decisive action to end honour-based violence because of 'political correctness' and because they are afraid of being accused of racism or 'Islamophobia'. The government has some legitimate concerns about how to approach this issue; few communities respond favourably if they believe that an alien value system is being forced upon them. The government must therefore make clear that it is not seeking to enforce conformity, assimilation or 'western' values but rather that it is promoting ideas of women's rights and sexual equality that are universal. Political leaders also need to say that in Britain's pluralistic society all individuals and groups have an obligation to stand up for all the rights of all society's members and to fight violence and injustice wherever it occurs. Politicians must recognise that not standing up for the rights of ethnic minority women is racism; it is to say that immigrant women feel pain, humiliation and fear less than native Britons and that they should not aspire to the freedom that they would want for themselves; it is to say that they are less human for being part of a foreign culture. The government must show that it believes that all women should have the right to choose their own futures regardless of the culture of their parents and community; similarly to proclaim that the desire to live free of violence and servitude, fear and intimidation is not a 'western' trait but one that is common to all people.

Appendix

A letter from the 'Muslim Wellwishers Group'

Cardiff-based community group's circular which went to more than 1,250 Pakistani Muslim homes in Cardiff, according to Shahen Taj, the director of the Henna Foundation in the city. The document appears to have been sent with the aim of discouraging individuals and families from acting in ways which the community believes to be immoral. The following text appears with its original spelling and punctuation.

PRIVATE AND CONFIDENTIAL

Dear Mrs. Shahnaz Tariq,

Do the community's respectable women really know who you are, and the family that you belong to?

Shahnaz (Sadiq) Tariq (wife of Mohammed Tariq Grocer / Off Licensee, Clifton, Cardiff)

Shahnaz is a woman who was forced into an arranged marriage to a man called Mohammed Tariq of spar Shop a Grocer / Off Licensee.

The sad thing is that once someone is forced into an arranged marriage there is no turning back unless a woman is strong and puts principles before any other thing, which Shahnaz has shown.

This particular lady enjoyed the best part of her life as a child with her family and then growing up to the High School days. These are all precious mischief sweet memories that she has experienced in her six form days at Hawardian, which were abruptly brought to an end when the family realised she was not excelling at academics, but was only enjoying and very much looking forward to school life. Forcibly arranging her marriage to Mohammed Tariq, the father thought was a right thing to do as the girl well into her puberty.

For Mohammed Tariq this was a passport to paradise, as in Pakistan he was suffering like any other peasants cutting corns in the field, milking cows and listening to flute music in the fields, and in the evenings the social past time was gossiping and back biting. When the opportunity came to come to Britain and the prospect of a British passport he could not believe his luck. Once the mattiage was arranged for whatever reason Mohammed Tariq resented Shahnaz and disliked her as this wasn't a love marriage, but forced, but what he did love was the opportunity to come to Britain and getting his hands on a British passport. The only thing that kept together was the British passport. Whilst waiting for a passport his careless and laid back approach produced children, as a result of this he has always felt that he is trapped, since he was never happy with what Shahnaz had to offer him. He always thought that the grass was definitely greener elsewhere and therefore he has never stopped searching for illicit sexual affairs, and hoping that he may find something that his was unable to give him.

It's impossible to feel sorry for Shahnaz as she has became similar to gangsters mole and disgust is an everyday occurrence which she has become to accept as a norm of life.

Shahnaz has been surrounded for the best part of her life by members of her family who were either, accused of adultery, indecently assaulting children or those arrested for gang rape of an underage girls, or selling alcohol to underage children, which was also charged with herself.

Shahnaz's father Haji Mohammed Sadiq was arrested recently for indecently assaulting children, as a result of this he very seldom comes out for fear of persecution, and is currently planning to leave the country.

Shahnaz's brother Mahmood Sadiq also known as Moody, of Bayside Chip Shop, was arrested and found guilty for gang raping a young underage girl for which he was given a lengthy prison sentence, and will remain on the sex offenders register for the rest of his life.

Shahnaz's brother-in-law Asif of Spar Shop Grange Town, was also arrested for indecently assaulting the young girl. When arrested he was asked: "why did you put your hand in the young girls panties?" "He replied I was looking for the chocolate that I thought she had taken without paying."

Shahnaz's husband Mohammed Tariq is notorious for his evil behaviour in the community. He is accused by the community for his adultery of which his wife is fully aware, she has fought on many occasions with Pakistani ladies whom she blamed he was having affairs with behind her back. Her husband who wants to be on the mosque committee as well as earning his living from selling alcohol, he went beyond the boundaries of decency and sold alcohol to underage children, for which he was charged together with his wife. He struck a deal with the prosecuting authorities by asking them that he will plead guilty of they would drop the charges against his wife for the same offence that they both committed. The authorities accepted his request. He was found to have broken the law on two occasions and was found guilty and heavily fined, therefore having a criminal record. Mohammed Tariq is a known bad man who looks at other people's mothers, sisters, daughters and wives with lusting evil eyes. This fact is well known in the community; even a poet wrote a complete poem on Mohammed Tariq entitled 'The Zan', officially branding him in the community as 'The Adulterer".

Mohammed Tariq ha been pleased that the poet has made him famous within the community, as The Zani. This has been proved by the fact that he is happy with the contents of the poem he has not challenged the work of the poet, who has immortalised him in Cardiff as 'The Zani'.

Shahnaz's husband Mohammed Tariq has recently declared that a mosque belongs to him and his limited company, and not to the members of the public who have been donating money in their hundreds and thousands over two decades. A statement like this is normally made by kafirs (non-believers), those who seek hell on earth, as well as their ultimate reward in the life after which also will be hell.

No genuine Muslim or a person who honour the respect of their mother, sister, daughter or wife will allow them near Mohammed Tariq's home or his family, unless they have no gherrat (honour). No honourable lady who has respect and honour will lend her name to the evil homemade Mohammed Tariq and Co. Organisation called 'hope' (umeed).

Recently Mohammed Tariq and his accomplice who has been branded as the Abra of Cardiff (evil tyrant who tried to take over Mecca), have hot together after failing in all their endeavours, and come up with their final idea to form a women's group and call it 'Hope' (umeed). This was the idea of the man who was called Abra of Cardiff and Mohammed Tariq who has been branded 'The Zani'.

Both of these men together with their blind and illiterate followers who are easily led, are now putting forward their final objective, which is to make the women carry out their evil plans, as they have faied so miserably to do anything over many yearts.

For many years Mohammed Tariq together with his accomplice, one calling himself General Secretary and one calling himself Chairman, have been misleading the community with the support of the sacrificial goats who have no directions or objectives other than to make money and put it in their shoe boxes or under the mattress. The so called "Jacos donkeys" are now supporting Mohammed Tariq by allowing him to make his wife Chairman of "Hope", and supporting Abra for Abra's wife to be General Secretary of 'Hope'.

What a farce!

No educated god fearing true carers, respectable and honourable members of the community will support these people once the truth is before them. Which decent and honourable man will allow his children or his wife to be befriended by Mohammed Tariq's wife Shahnaz, so that she can take these women home for her husband to ogle over with his evil and sinister dirty looks and thoughts that are perverted?

Just as Mohammed Tariq and accomplice have been baffling and making a fool of fools, sometimes genuine people have been mislead too, who have been made into bulls, owls and donkeys. In the same way Mohammed Tariq and his accomplice want their wives to do the same as they have been doing for over 15 years, which is to hoodwink women by feeding them lies, intimidating them and trying to treat them as cows, owls and stray cats.

Mohammed Tariq'a wife Shahnaz recently made her maiden statement as a bogus Chairman of the homemade society of Mohammed Tariq's and his accomplice, the statement she made was as follows:

'I want my partco opened".

The members of the mosque were reluctant to open "Shahnaz's partco" as she put it, as she had no right to give consent, especially when her husband had failed to open it. Why was she flaunting her request around the city?

The members of the community were quite concerned as to why Shahnaz was continuously using the phrase:

" I want my partco opened."

Why would she want partco opened? Surely the area to which

she was referring to was too small. But she was still adamant that she wanted her partco opened.

Members of the community decided that in order to keep her happy and satisfy her, some volunteers went in with full force and opened partco; they were amazed that the area was not as small as members thought.

So what is the purpose of this organisation called 'Hope' (umeed)?

Hope is an organisation made up by Mohammed Tariq, husband of Shahnaz, and the Abra, husband of the Secretary, to use these women and the member ladies who are being asked to sign the membership forms, as human shields, for when they do battle with people who are true champions of the community, the ones who will never sit back and allow Mohammed Tatiq and Abra to succeed, to use when the good men of God come to beat evil, these women will be used by this evil pair, to take them on. How degrading to treat the decent respectable mothers, sisters, daughters and wives in this way.

What 'Hope' has Shahnaz got in trying to resolve community issues, when she is living with people who are probably the worst individuals any family can have, this woman surrounded by these so called men, she is trying to please them, what example is she setting, aren't you supposed to judge the company you keep?

'HOPE' (umeed)

Maybe she has 'Hope' that her father is never involved with young children again.

Maybe she has 'Hope' that her brother does not gang rape anyone underage again.

Maybe she has 'Hope' that her brother-in-law does not put hands in places that are criminal, involving children.

Maybe she has 'Hope' and her biggest hope yet that her husband may lose his eyesight so that he does not have preying eyes on other people's mothers, sisters, daughters and wives.

Maybe she has 'Hope' that her husband does not ask her to befriend other women under the umbrella of 'Hope', and bring them to the home as victims.

Maybe she has 'Hope' that someone will day again marry Azra, her sister, even though she has a past with a man from Riverside who had been showing her around Cardiff for approximately 3 years and her family refused to allow this gentleman from the Riverside community to marry her.

How can this woman Shahnaz stand up and call herself Chairman when she has no hope in hell? And can't even sort out her own family affairs?

Who would trust their children, mothers, sisters, daughters and wives in her home, where all the four beasts have access?

The community is well aware that many genuine ladies have signed membership forms and become members of 'Hope', innocently supporting these evil men and the endeavours of Mohammed Tariq and the Abra of Cardiff – Allah will never help succeed these men and women with their evil intentions.

We pray that the mothers, sisters, daughters and wives completely disassociate themselves from this organisation 'Hope' (umeed), which is being launched by Mohammed Tariq, and his co-conspirators.

We request those respectable, honourable God fearing ladies whose husbands are true men and not idiots, bulls, owls or donkeys to kindly refrain from joining 'Hope' (umeed) and if you have already joined, withdraw your so called membership in the interest of izzat, honour, respect and dignity for yourself, your husband, your children and your family as a whole in the community.

The true hope is that after reading this the respectable ladies will completely disengage themselves from this sinister society of women prepared to serve certain evil men, and be used and humiliated.

Do not allow your mothers, sisters, daughters, wives and children to fall into the preying eyes of evil men, who will use their wives, mothers, sisters and daughters to get into your homes to achieve their dirty deeds.

There is one thing that must be brought to the attention of the dear respected ladies, which is, when at first a few years ago a women's organisation was formed, Mohammed Tariq and the so-called Abra condemned those poor ladies who were and are doing a worthy job to help suppressed ladies. Mohammed Tariq and Abra called these ladies because they formed an organisation of women, prostitutes, home wreckers, and women that wear

trousers and their husbands wear skirts (stockings and red sti-
lettos). Today, these very so called men are now promoting the
same thing that they were against. Why have Mohammed Tariq
and Abra got no shame left in their body; what will these women
be called in their eyes?

Is it because Mohammed Tariq has never had any respect and his
co-conspirators in particularly Abra that they now want to bring
shame on other people's mothers, sisters, daughters and wives?
O Brothers of Islam, in particularly Pakistani Brothers, protect
your Iszat, form these evil men, and their evil women, who are
now out to mislead you, they are all as the poet of Cardiff said,
'Abra's Army' (kaffirs) (Non-believers).

Please note: currently being prepared is a detailed report on those
women who are conspiring with the evil men who have brought
shame upon their family, their religion, their community and
themselves. They will be exposed so that we can protect our true
mothers, sisters, daughters and wives who are honourable, and
respectable in our community.

A detailed report is also being compiled on Abra and how he has
rewarded Mohammed Tariq for bringing shame and dishonour
to women in his family. When the Abra report is out these ladies
names will be disclosed.

The saddest thing is that Abra instead of punishing Mohammed
Tariq, had no other alternative but to award him because he is
70+ and there is no-man in his family who is prepared to challenge Mohammed Tariq. Instead men in his family go and clean
his shoes and sing his praise out of fear in case he exposes details
about their women and what he got up to in his continental style
butchery shop. All will be exposed in full soon.

Mohammed Tariq and Abra will be punished in this life and
hereafter, for their sins. The time has come for them both to pay
back the community, for using them and misusing them. God is
aware and the community is aware of the Shetan's (devils) who
support them, just like blind pigs with no directions, morals or
values, they will also be punished by God.

Mohammed Tariq achievements have been stated above and finally to conclude this please note that he has recently been arrested on tow occasions for assaulting Mosque Officials for which
he spent all day in Police custody. Instead of punishing him 'Jaco
and his donkeys' spent all day trying to free him.

He is currently being investigated by the Police complaint Authority at the highest level. He is currently being investigated by a very serious branch of the police for fraud together with others for trying to obtain money of mosque by deception (insurance fraud).

O good Muslim, Pakistani Brothers, protect the honour of your loved ones from Mohammed Tariq, bogus secretary and Abra bogus Chairman and now Mohammed Tariq's wife Shahnaz Sadiq Tariq Chairman, and Abra's wife Secretary of 'Hope', same snakes same skins (wolves in sheep's clothing).

God will help us defeat them at every opportunity, as Mohammed Tariq and his co-conspirators intentions are pure evil. The Abra Army was defeated once before and shall be defeated once again inshallah.

Thank you

Muslim Wellwishers Group

Bibliography

Chapter I:

Holy, Ladislav, Kinship: Honour and Solidarity: Cousin marriage in the Middle East (Manchester University Press, Manchester, 1989).

Peristiany, J G (ed.), Honour and Shame: The values of Mediterranean Society (University of Chicago, Chicago 1966; London 1974).

Wahud, Anima, Inside the Gender Jihad: Women's Reform in Islam, Oneworld Publications (Oxford, 2006)

Chapter 2:

Raleigh, V.S., and Balarajan, R, 'Suicide and Self-Burning among Indians and West Indians in England and Wales', British Journal of Psychiatry, 129, pp.365-368 (1992).

Chapter 5:

Lightfoot-Klein, Hammy, 'The Sexual Experience and Marital Adjustment of Genitally Circumcised and Infibulated Females in the Sudan', The Journal of Sex Research, 26, 3, pp. 375-392 (August 1989).

Momoh, Comfort (ed.), Female Genital Mutilation (Radcliffe Publishing, 2005).

Roald, Anne Sofie, Women in Islam: The Western Experience (Routledge, London, 2001).

Acknowledgements

Abigail Morris, Jewish Woman's Aid
Amtal Rana, Kiran Asian Women Aid
Andrew Cameron, Metropolitan Police
Anne Marie Hutchinson, Dawson Cornwell
Atif Imtiaz, community worker in Bradford
Batool Al- Toma, the National Muslim Women's Advisory Group
Bawjit Banga, Newham Asian Woman's Refuge
Bawjit Singh, social worker
Catherine Hossain, Muslim Public Affairs Committee (MPACUK)
Debbie Fawcett, Hyndburn and Ribble Valley Outreach women's
    group
Diana Nammi, Iranian and Kurdish Women's Rights Organisation
Ila Patel, Asha Project
Ena Mercy, Pennines Domestic Violence group
Fathiya Yusuf, Refuge
Frank Field, MP
Ghayasuddin Siddiqui, Muslim Parliament
Ghazala Khan, Naye Subah
Ghazala Razzaq, Roshni Asian Women's Resource Centre
    (Sheffield)
Gina Khan
Gona Saed, Middle East Centre for Women's Rights
Grace Busuttil North Kirlees Refuge near Leeds
Haley, Jewish Woman's Aid
Hassan Safour, Muslim Welfare House
Humera Khan, An-Nisa Society
Ibrahim Mogra, Muslim Council of Britain
Ishbana Hussain, Staying Put Project
Jasvinder Sanghera, Shazia Qayum and Imran Rehman, Karma
    Nirvana
Jatinder Chana, Asha Projects
Jenny Moody, Luton Women's Aid
John Paton, Lancashire Family Mediation Service,
Judy Morgan, Lantern Project
Julie Pyke, Annah
Kirklees Asian Black Women's Welfare Association (KABBWA)
Kubir Randhawa, Asian Family Counseling Service
Lesley Musa, Women's Aid (Glasgow)
Latifa Rahman, Hackney Asian Women's Aid
Manjit Kaur, Roshni (Birmingham)

Maureen Salmon, Forward
Mohamed Baleela, Domestic Violence intervention Project
Mona Elogeali, Al Husaniya Morrocan Women's group
Muna Choudhury, Ashram Housing Association (Birmingham)
Narinder Matharoo, Sikh Sangat London East temple (Leyton)
Nazir Afzal, Crown Prosecution Service
Nicola Sharp and Derya Yildirim, Refuge
Nisha Kapoor, University of Manchester
Olivia Madden, Panah
Omar Yasin Ibrahim, Islington Somali Community Centre
Philip Balmforth, Bradford police service
Rafaat Mughal, Joint Association of Nissa Trusts
Rahni Binjie and Tanisha Jnagel, Roshni Asian women's aid
Rania Hafez, University of East London
Rehana Bibi, Hyndburn and Ribble Valley Outreach (Accrington)
Saba Melles, Eritrean Community centre
Sajidah Naseem, translator
Sana Bukhari, Ashiana (Sheffield)
Sawsan Selim, Kurdish Refugee Women's Association
Shahien Taj, Henna Foundation
Shaminder Ubhi, Ashiana
Sharmien Khan, Annah project
Sheikh Barakutullah
Sheikh Haitham al-Haddad, Sharia Council
Southall Black Sisters
Waheed Malik, Awaaz Asian Women's Group
Walik Moustafa
Yasin Ibrahim, Islington Somali Community Centre
Yasmin Rehman Association of Chief Police Officers (ACPO)
Zahia Tatimahand, Kiran Asian Women's Aid
Zalkha Ahmed, Apna Haq

'Ayesha'
'Ibn Qazi', former member of al-Muhajiroun and Hizb ut-Tahrir
Jas
'Latifa
"Mohammed"
Raj
'Saamiya'
'Sakina'
Shagufta
Rukhsana
'Rosi'

Joshua Segal, Tom Woods, Ed van der Byl-Knoefel, Cem Suleiman,
    Hannah Stuart and all the staff at Civitas.

The authors would also like to thank all those women who were
interviewed for this report and do not wish to be named or quoted.

The Centre for Social Cohesion

The Centre for Social Cohesion is a non-partisan thinktank that was set up by Civitas in 2007 to examine issues related to community cohesion in Britain. Headquartered in London, it was founded to promote new thinking that can help bring Britain's ethnic and religious communities closer together while strengthening British traditions of openness, tolerance and democracy.

James Brandon is a Senior Research Fellow at the Centre for Social Cohesion.

Salam Hafez is a Senior Research Fellow at the Centre for Social Cohesion.